BETTER SAFE Than SORRY

Real-life stories, tips, and more—a guide to everyday safety

Compiled by Mike Atnip

© 2022 by TGS International, a wholly owned subsidiary of Christian Aid Ministries, Berlin, Ohio.

All rights reserved. No part of this book may be reproduced or stored in any retrieval system, in any form or by any means, electronic or mechanical, without written permission from the publisher except for brief quotations embodied in critical articles and reviews.

ISBN: 978-1-63813-093-2
Cover and text layout design: Kristi Yoder
Printed in China

Published by:
TGS International
P.O. Box 355
Berlin, Ohio 44610 USA
Phone: 330.893.4828
Fax: 330-893-4893
www.tgsinternational.com

BETTER SAFE Than SORRY

Real-life stories, tips, and more—a guide to everyday safety

Compiled by Mike Atnip

Table of Contents

Introduction 7

Home and Community Safety 13
   Bomb in the Basement . . . and on the Stove 13
   Burned in the Bathtub 16
   Just a Pot of Hot Water 18
   Click! Went the Latch 21
   Watch Those Stairs! 23
   A Little Boy . . . on a Little Mower 25
   No Treats, Please! 27
   Keep Medicines Up and Away! 28
   Are Accidents God's Will? 30
   Are There Exceptions to Safety Rules? 32
   Little Bad Batteries 33
   Kill Those Germs—Before They Kill You 34
   Fun on the Ice 38
   Water: Friend and Foe 41
   Batter Up . . . Pitcher Down! 48
   Kidnapping—Mom's Greatest Fear 50

Fire Safety 55
   Scorched Kitchen for Breakfast 55
   Don't Burn the House with the Hotdogs! 59
   Firing Up the Old Wood Stove 60
   House Fires: Dark, Quick, and Deadly 63
   Fire Extinguishers?—Give Me Four of Them! 66
   Please Set My House on Fire! 70
   Sprayed by Hot Foam 73
   The Candle That Lit the Island 74
   Chimney Fires 76

Farm and Logging Safety 81
   Blinded by His Own Knife 81
   Where Are the Children? 82
   Bulls, Rams, and Bucks 84
   Almost Gassed to Death 87
   Dilemma in the Manure Pit 90
   Grain Engulfment: It Only Takes Two Seconds 93
   Burned by the Drinking Cup 97

- Crushed Head . . . and Heart! ... 100
- Rolled Alive ... 103
- Skid-Steer Monsters ... 104
- When Can Johnny Drive the Tractor? ... 106
- It Didn't Stop! ... 107
- Just a Little Hydraulic Oil ... 108
- Tractor Rollovers ... 109
- Prepare to Meet Thy God . . . While Plowing ... 112
- PTOs—People-Tangling Objects ... 113
- Praises in the Woods ... 116
- Watching Out for Those with Disabilities ... 121

Shop and Construction Safety ... 123
- Why You Don't Read Safety Warnings ... 123
- Knot in the Eye ... 124
- Hastening to Cut Off His Thumb ... 126
- A Safer Table Saw ... 127
- Walter's Welding Woes ... 130
- *K-THUMP!* ... 134
- Stretching Your Ladder ... 136
- Did You Say Hearing Safety? ... 139

Gun/Hunting Safety ... 145
- *POW!* ... 145
- Boys and Guns ... 148
- Don't Fall for Venison! ... 150
- Sharpen That Knife! ... 152

Road Safety ... 155
- Three Glasses in a Backpack ... 155
- Flipped by the Gravel ... 157
- Thinking Deeply and Broadly About Safety ... 158
- Two-Wheeled Safety ... 162
- E-Bikes: More Power = Harder Wrecks ... 166
- Pedestrian Safety—Mom Was Right! ... 168
- Avoiding the Grave—Be Seen! ... 169
- No Time to Tie the Horse ... 171
- SMV—Sign of Multi-Use Versatility? ... 172
- A New Pony Cart ... 174
- To Be Seen or Not to Be Seen? ... 176
- Consistency in Road Safety ... 178
- When Being Right Is Dead Right ... 181
- ATV + ROV = 2 Funerals/Day ... 183

Endnotes ... 187
Photo Credits ... 189
About the Author ... 191

Introduction

Oh, no—not another boring safety book!
I can easily imagine that if I were a student again at my desk in third grade with Mrs. Miller as my teacher, I would probably groan inside—possibly even audibly—if she announced, "Time for safety class. Please pull out your safety books."

This book is *not* just another safety book with long lists of dos and don'ts. This is a book of real-life stories—stories that happened to people like John, Peter, Susan, and Martha . . . and could happen to *you*.

The most important safety book
Did you know that the Bible is a safety book? Included in the Bible are many stories of people who did unsafe things and suffered horribly for their bad decisions. While many of these stories are about spiritual safety, others are about physical safety.

The word *salvation* is related to safety. A person who violates a safety rule and gets himself into a tough situation needs to be saved from that situation. Those who walk in the commandments of God have spiritual safety assured them.

This book focuses on physical safety more than spiritual safety. We might wonder if God cares about our physical safety. Yes, He does. The Law of Moses included a number of safety practices among its many laws. Let's take a look at one of them—in Deuteronomy 22:8:

> When thou buildest a new house, then thou shalt make a battlement for thy roof, that thou bring not blood upon thine house, if any man fall from thence.

While this law has a spiritual lesson in it, it is also a very basic safety rule, or ordinance. It tells us that whoever builds a house is at least somewhat responsible for the safety of anyone who lives in or visits the house. Therefore, God's law required the owner of the house to put a low wall around the roof. We know, of course, that most of the roofs at that time and place were flat roofs. People walked on them and used them as living spaces. Can you imagine going to visit a friend with your family and finding out that your visit would take place on a flat roof with no wall or railing around the edge? It could seem exciting at first to peek over the edge to the street below. But what about your little brother or sister who is just learning to crawl? Would not common sense tell us that it is unsafe to be on a flat roof without any railing around it?

Safety = common sense

Putting a wall around a flat roof is really just common sense, right? So why do we so often need safety reminders? Is common sense not enough?

Well, ask any of the people in the stories of this book if they would not have appreciated a simple warning before they lost a loved one or were perhaps seriously injured themselves.

Beyond common sense

You may have read some really ridiculous warning labels. Let's look at a few. These are real examples, and it is okay to snicker.

- On the bar of a chainsaw—*Do not hold the wrong end of a chainsaw.*
- On a heating torch—*Contents may catch fire.*

Does an egg carton really need a warning that it may contain eggs?

- On an egg carton—*This product may contain eggs.*
- On a letter opener—*Safety glasses recommended.*
- On a scooter—*This product moves when used.*
- On a box of sleeping pills—*May cause drowsiness.*
- On a wheelbarrow—*Not intended for highway use.*
- On a package of fireplace logs—*Caution: risk of fire.*
- On a clothes hanger—*Caution: Do not swallow.*

The problem is that some people will sue manufacturers for things that go wrong when they fail to use simple common sense when using the product. Why would anyone, for example, hold on to the bar of a chainsaw while trying to cut firewood? Why would anyone need safety glasses when using a letter opener? And doesn't everyone know you don't eat clothes hangers?

When Moses told the children of Israel that the owner of a house is responsible to put a low wall around a flat roof, he didn't tell them to also include a warning sign on the wall: *Warning: Do not jump over wall!*

Practicing safety does not need to include silly warnings that ignore common sense. But we are all human, and reminders to pay attention to real dangers are sometimes needed to stir up our sleepy minds.

Fear

Then there is fear. From my childhood I remember the story of Chicken Little, who was forever scared that the sky was falling down. A good, healthy sense of fear in dangerous situations is built into us by God Himself. That is why you cling more tightly to a tree's branches as you climb higher. A natural, healthy fear of heights is just good, old-fashioned common sense.

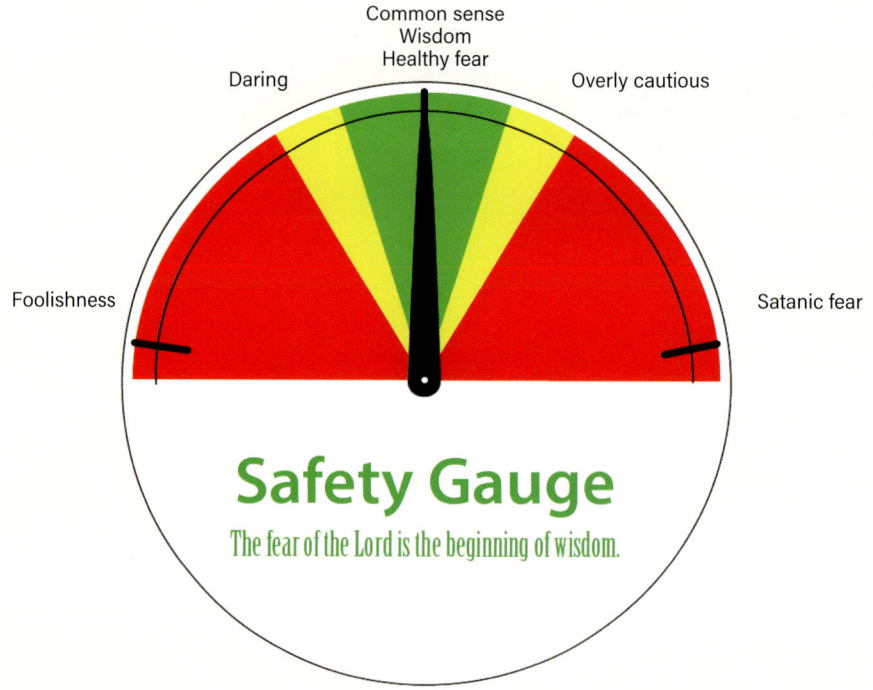

There is, however, a fear that is not healthy—such as a fear that the sky is falling down. This fear is a constant nagging in your mind that something bad is going to happen—somehow, some way, and probably today. This unhealthy—shall I call it ungodly?—fear is what causes someone to refuse to go outside after dark or be afraid to climb a ladder more than a step or two. These fears are unrealistic and can tower over people like a monster and prevent them from living a life of common sense.

Wisdom

So what is the difference between standing on the top of a wobbly ten-foot stepladder and being afraid to go up more than two steps on a solid one? Again, we are back to common sense and wisdom.

Wisdom is the ability to use knowledge—and common sense—in the correct way. We use a ladder to reach high places. We know that if a ladder is in good condition, it is a valuable tool. We also know that standing on the top step of a stepladder is much more dangerous than standing two steps farther down. Both wisdom and common sense tell us not to stand on that top step.

But wisdom also tells us that if a house is burning down it is perfectly fine to use the top step—even if it is dangerous— if that is the only way to escape the fire.

Foolishness

The opposite of wisdom is foolishness. Foolishness ignores common sense and knowledge. Satan tempted Jesus to leap off the temple in Jerusalem as a way to test God. Jesus was wise enough to know that even though God could keep him from getting hurt, He did not want to be tested like that. Jesus also knew that Satan is a liar, so He used wisdom and did not listen to him.

We know that people who get hurt often do so because they act foolishly. When wisdom and common sense are put aside, danger is often lurking nearby. As you read the stories in this book, see if you can spot a point where the people involved cast aside wisdom and common sense. Many of these stories involve someone who chose a foolish action, often without thinking.

Choose wisdom

Safety, then, is wisdom. The Bible exhorts us in Proverbs 4:5 to, "Get wisdom, get understanding: forget it not." We could paraphrase this verse as, "Practice safety, use common sense, and don't forget it!"

Many people have offered to share their stories in this book. Although names have been changed, every story is true and is about a real person just like you. These people have humbly offered their mistakes to teach you to love wisdom. Some carry scars and pain, both in their bodies and in their hearts.

May they not share their stories in vain.

Home and Community Safety

Bomb in the Basement . . . and on the Stove

Most homes in the United States have a potential bomb within them: the common water heater. An overheated water heater has been known to explode, flying up to three hundred feet into the air.

But don't lose any sleep over this fact. Although a water heater does occasionally explode, it is very rare. Let's look at why a water heater can potentially become a safety threat.

It's called *steam*. Yes, steam is a very powerful force. When water turns to steam, it expands 1,600 times in terms of volume. That means that one gallon of water, which takes up only a little over ⅛ cubic foot, needs 212 cubic feet when it turns to steam. If it does not have that much area, it will build up pressure.

To put this in more practical terms, let's say you have a bedroom that measures ten feet by ten feet by eight feet. To find the volume of the room, we multiply these three numbers, which equals 800 cubic feet of space.

If one gallon of water expands to 212 cubic feet when turned to steam, then four gallons of water would be all it would take to fill your bedroom with steam.

The problem is that a typical water heater holds about forty gallons. This means that if the water in the water heater suddenly turns to steam, it needs ten bedrooms in order to have enough space. But what if it has only a forty-gallon tank into which it can expand?

The answer is that when forty gallons of water turns into steam inside a forty-gallon tank, the tank will likely explode from the pressure. Of course, if a pressure relief valve is installed on the water heater, the pressure will gradually be released and no explosion will occur. However, if the forty gallons of water instantly turns to steam, the explosive power is equal to about two-thirds of a stick of dynamite. If you think of a stick of dynamite going off in your water heater, you might be able to imagine the tank flying up like a rocket, bursting through the floor, the ceiling, and the roof. Yes, it has happened, but it is very rare, thanks to pressure relief valves. Always remember:

- Never remove or plug the relief valve on a water heater. If it is leaking, make sure to replace it.
- Never build a heated water system (hot water through a wood stove, for example) without installing a pressure relief valve in the system.

Steam engines

A few people still use steam engines, although they are mainly used for demonstrations at antique shows. There is a reason—a good reason—why steam engine use is often highly regulated by the government. In the days when they were common sources of power, many deaths and injuries occurred. Instead of a quart of water in a pressure cooker—or forty gallons in a water heater—steam engines often contain hundreds of gallons of water.

As pressure builds upon water, the boiling point goes up. Normally, water boils at about 212°F. But at fifteen pounds of pressure, water boils at about 250°F. At seventy pounds of pressure, the boiling temperature rises to 316°F.

Let's imagine a steam engine running seventy pounds of pressure. The water in the boiler is at 250°F, with a little bit at a time being injected through the firebox, where it heats up to 316°F, turns to steam, and creates pressure. Now let's imagine that somewhere in the system a leak suddenly develops. The pressure in the whole system drops to zero, or normal.

What would happen?

Instantly, every drop of water that is hotter than 212°F would turn to steam—and expand 1,600 times! As the hot water expands into steam, nearby water that was initially cooler than 212°F may also suddenly be heated to the boiling point, making that explode into steam as well. If you can imagine several hundred gallons of water instantaneously expanding 1,600 times, you can imagine a boiler explosion. The picture below shows an example of the power of uncontrolled steam. In this case, one train engine was blown into the air and landed on top of another. Thankfully, this incident, which occurred in Norway in 1897, did not result in any injuries or deaths. Unfortunately, that was not always the case.

One of the most gruesome accounts is of a steam engine that blew up near Walnut Creek, Ohio, on February 23, 1882. This blast killed four men and injured two others. The force of the blast sent pieces of the boiler flying as far as neighboring farms and tore off body parts of the two men working closest to the boiler. This steam engine was being used to power a sawmill. Apparently the safety valve was not working properly, and the pressure became too much for the corroded boiler.

Steam engine explosions still occur occasionally, and deaths still happen from them. In 2001, a Case 110 steam tractor blew up in Medina, Ohio, killing five people. Debris flew up to one hundred yards in all directions. An investigation revealed that some of the metal of the engine had corroded away, leaving it too weak to withstand the high pressure.

Steam in the kitchen

Very few people tinker with steam engines these days. However, many homes have a smaller version of a potential steam bomb that they use every summer: it's called a pressure cooker or canner. Although newer models come with several safety features—with a minimum of two safety relief valves, if not three—older models may not. When pressure canners first gained popularity in the 1940s and 1950s, some manufacturers built canners that were simply not safe, and pressure canners soon received a reputation for blowing off their tops. Today, however, pressure canner explosions are rare, but that is no reason to ignore the following safety practices:

- Have your pressure cooker's relief valve checked regularly. Some state extension offices provide this service every canning season. A pressure cooker can become a mini-bomb if the relief valve is not functioning properly. Remember, if the boiling water in the pressure cooker suddenly turns to steam, it needs 1,600 times the space to expand!

- Let the canner cool sufficiently before opening the lid. In most cases, opening the canner too quickly will not cause it to blow up, but it may blow out scalding steam—enough to give serious burns.

- Check for damage or wear before every canning season. Has a mouse chewed the gasket? Has the gauge rusted so that it is no longer accurate? Remember, a damaged pressure canner may do more than ruin your batch of green beans—it could cause serious burns or injury.

Burned in the Bathtub

Splish! Splash! What could be more delightful for two-year-old Betsie and six-month-old Jennie than playing in a bathtub of warm water?

Baths are a regular routine in most homes, and Linda had put the two smallest children in the tub and was letting them enjoy themselves. At that moment her husband Joseph came into the house asking for help with several cows that were causing trouble in the barn.

Linda asked seven-year-old Julie to watch over the little ones and quickly headed for the barn. Julie soon took baby Jennie out of the tub and dressed her, then decided to take her along out to the barn to see what was happening.

In the busyness of tending to emergencies, time often slips by faster than we realize. When the needs in the barn were finally taken care of, Linda headed for the house. Before she even got there, she heard screams coming out the door!

Her maternal instincts kicking in, Linda was soon in the bathroom. She was shocked to see Betsie standing there pulling at her feet . . . and tearing off loose skin.

Little Betsie had turned on the hot water, which was still running when Linda arrived. Thankfully, Betsie had not fallen into the scalding water or sat down in it. One foot was damaged worse than the other, probably because of that foot being in the hot water longer than the other when she climbed out of the tub.

Immediately Linda put both injured feet into cool water. After getting her daughter dressed, she wrapped her feet in a soft towel before heading for the local hospital. A few spots on poor Betsie's feet suffered third-degree burns, but no skin grafting was required. Normal burn procedures were used, and Betsie's feet healed well.

Today, twenty-five years later, Betsie has scarred feet, but she can use them normally. A lesson was burned into Linda's heart that day: *Never leave a small child unattended in a bathtub!*

Hot water safety

All modern household water heaters have temperature adjustments. Having extremely hot water available from the tap may be useful in certain situations, but we must remember that such hot water can cause burns. Ask Betsie if you do not believe it! Although it may seem inconvenient, keeping the water heater set at a safe temperature level is the wise thing to do. If hotter water is needed, heat it on the stove.

Water at 125° Fahrenheit (52° Celsius) can cause skin burns after a couple of minutes. Children have thinner skin than adults and burn more easily. For this reason, most safety guides recommend turning water heaters down to 120°F (49°C) or lower. Newer water heaters usually have settings marked on the thermostat. Older water heaters may need to be set with a thermometer placed under the spigot. If you check the water temperature with a thermometer, let the hot water run for a minute or two before taking a measurement.

Bathtub safety

- Never allow small children to bathe without supervision.
- Install grab bars for the elderly as they can easily slip in a bathtub or shower and be unable to lift themselves back up.
- Check the water temperature of your water heater—today!

I knew the hot water was truly hot in our house. While writing this article, I decided to check it with a thermometer. Whoa! 139.1°F! Checking the thermostat on the water heater, I soon found out why: the thermostat was set to maximum temperature—150°F! Yes, I turned it down!

Just a Pot of Hot Water

Sam took his two-and-a-half-year-old daughter Amanda with him to the basement one evening to prepare some bath water. Because they lived in a house with no water heater, they heated their bath water on a stove and carried it to a plastic washtub. Without thinking too much about it, Sam set a large stockpot of steaming hot water on the floor so he could rinse the washtub first. Amanda held the flashlight.

"Amanda, can I please have the flashlight?" Sam asked. Amanda dutifully handed it to her father, and he began to rinse the washtub.

Suddenly Sam heard a gasp. No one really knows exactly how it happened, but somehow Amanda had dumped the gallon and a half of almost-boiling water over the front of her body. More than 50 percent of her body had second-degree to fourth-degree burns, with her arms and legs receiving the worst of it.

Ruby, her mother, was upstairs and heard Amanda's screams. "What's wrong?" she called down the stairs. Sam quickly pulled off Amanda's clothes and carried her up the stairs to the kitchen sink, which happened to have some cool water in it. He quickly put Amanda into the sink. Sitting in the cool water, Sam heard Amanda say, "Jesus, help me!" He realized that his daughter was in tremendous pain.

Taking Amanda out of the cool water, Sam quickly dried her off. His mind went to the Union salve they had in a nearby cabinet. By this time, large sheets of skin were hanging from her body. The sight was so ghastly that Ruby had to leave the room. Sam then smeared the salve over the burned parts of Amanda's body.

Sam and Ruby did not realize it at the time, but Amanda's body was starting to go into shock. They discussed what to do next. Should they try B&W salve, which often produced almost miraculous results, or should they seek conventional medical treatment? After some discussion, they decided they needed to do *something*—and *soon*. They were pretty sure the case was too serious for B&W, so they rushed toward the emergency room.

Sam called the hospital and told them they were on their way with a burn victim. The emergency personnel were waiting with open doors when they arrived. By now it was about 11 p.m. The local hospital, however, was not set up for such a serious burn case, so they gave Amanda morphine and rushed her to a larger hospital with a burn/trauma center.

Some burn victims experience severe shock that can be worse than the actual burns. This was Amanda's case, and a few days later her body started to shut down. As her blood pressure dropped to dangerously low levels, she was moved from the burn center to intensive care. The toxicity levels in her body were high because her kidneys and liver were not functioning well, and her colon actually died. This poisoned her system, so the doctors did emergency surgery to remove her colon. Fluids began to accumulate in her body, putting pressure on her heart, and she was very close to dying. Because of the burn damage, the fingers of her right hand were amputated.

Once the damaged parts of her body were removed, Amanda began the long, painful process of healing. Instead of being in the hospital for one month as the doctors originally estimated, she ended up being there for nearly three months.

Today Amanda has some skin grafts and some missing fingers, but in general she is a healthy and cheerful girl and can pretty much lead a normal life. But it was a long, hard journey! Always remember that a pot of hot water is not "just a pot of hot water."

Lessons for Sam

- Sam learned that the trauma caused by burns can be more serious than the actual burns. Severe burns can throw the rest of the body into shock, which then kills the person. In other words, the burns themselves do not kill, but the trauma to the body makes it simply shut down.

- Burns are unpredictable. The victim may get worse quickly as Amanda did, or the shock may not hit until a week later. The latter is actually more common.

- The degree of the burns cannot be determined immediately. Sam also had not known about fourth-degree burns. The degree of a burn is determined by how deep the damage is:

    » **First-degree burns** damage only the outer layer of skin. Sunburn is an example of this type of burn. Long-term damage is rare for first-degree burns, but there can be some pain involved.

    » **Second-degree burns** go through the top layer of skin and damage the bottom layer. These burns produce blisters and will hurt if you touch them. Second-degree burns are divided into superficial and deep burns. If the second layer of skin is burned only partway through (superficial), no scarring is likely to occur. But if the second layer is damaged almost completely (deep), a scar or permanent change of skin color will likely result.

» **Third-degree burns** fully destroy both layers of skin. These burns do not turn red but may appear as black, brown, yellow, or white. Think of third-degree burns as a burnt piece of toast that is charred all the way through. Third-degree burns are often less painful than first- and second-degree burns because the nerve endings have been damaged so much that they cannot transmit pain signals.

» **Fourth-degree burns** go all the way through both layers of skin and damage underlying tissue as well, sometimes including the muscles or bones.

- Post-trauma from burns can affect other family members mentally and emotionally. The family routine is broken, the siblings are sometimes without parents for days on end while the parents stay with the burn victim, and just the sight of the burns or the scars can affect other family members in negative ways.

- Don't set hot water on the floor or where children can reach it. Most likely, Sam subconsciously thought the pot of hot water would be on the floor for only a minute or two. Today Sam thinks about the danger of hot water even when he has a cup of hot tea in his hand. When he sets it down, he tends to put it toward the back of the countertop!

- Be careful about leaving pots and pans with hot food or water near the edge of tables and countertops where children could try to see what is in them. If they can't see what it contains, they might pull the pot/pan over, spilling the contents over themselves.

Click! Went the Latch

It was Sunday afternoon—a great time to relax. Six-year-old Anthony noted that some of the afghans and blankets had been taken out of his mother's cedar chest in the living room. Opening the lid, he slid into the cozy little nest. Such a nice place to lie down and daydream!

The problem was that the lid did not want to stay open. Using his foot, Anthony pushed the lid back up whenever it started to close. Several times he pushed it back up. Then it happened. *Click!* The lid shut and latched before Anthony was able to kick it back open.

His first instinct was to scream and bang the lid to alert his parents and siblings, who had been in the room. But Anthony decided to play it brave and just lie there, assuming that his family knew what had happened. *They are probably waiting on me to get scared and scream,* he thought. *I will be really brave.*

After a few minutes, it became obvious that no one was going to open the latch. What Anthony did not know was that the rest of the family had just left the room and gone into the kitchen. Desperation began to overcome him. Pushing with all his might, he found that he could not open the latch. He began to pound, kick, scream, cry—anything to get some attention.

If he pushed really hard, he could get one corner of the lid up just a crack and let in some light. Putting his nose near the crack, he tried to get some fresh air. The cedar smell was stronger than he had thought. But it was no use; the crack simply did not let in enough fresh air.

After trying for a while to pry open the lid or get some attention, Anthony finally just sank back in exhaustion. Sleep overcame him.

Meanwhile, his parents had gone upstairs for a Sunday afternoon nap. Awakening awhile later, his father got up to do the evening chores. Anthony's siblings, all younger, realized that Anthony was missing and asked Mom and Dad where he could be. But no one was really alarmed; a six-year-old in a large house could be in all kinds of places, happily playing.

Anthony's father headed downstairs. Normally he turned left at the bottom of the steps to go out the door to do his chores. But for some unknown reason, this time he turned right, into the living room.

Strange noises were coming from the area of the cedar chest. Had a cat gotten behind the furniture and was scratching around? Investigating further, he realized that the sounds were coming from the cedar chest. Opening the lid, he found Anthony—as white as a sheet!

Besides some headaches for the rest of the day, Anthony suffered no long-term harm. He does experience some claustrophobia at times, but that may be incidental. What would have happened had his father made the usual left turn at the bottom of the steps?

Anthony thanks God for that "unknown" impulse that caused his father to turn into the living room. Now, over two decades later, Anthony is married and has a family of his own. He makes sure to avoid any cedar chests with latches!

De-latching the home

Old appliances are more likely to have latches that cannot be opened from the inside. Children playing hide-and-seek have gotten trapped in old freezers or refrigerators on the junk pile, sometimes perishing when the latch locked them in.

Check your home, inside and out, for any appliances or storage containers that cannot be opened from the inside. While checking for these death traps, also consider the possibility of objects falling on the lid or door of a container, preventing it from being opened from the inside. For example, a wooden storage chest in a closet may not have a latch on it, but children playing hide-and-seek may crawl inside and inadvertently cause objects stacked on a nearby shelf to fall on the lid, preventing it from being opened.

Teach children the danger of getting locked in boxes and storage containers. Old cars may have trunks that could latch shut after a child crawls in. Hide-and-seek is a common game for children, but teach your children to hide safely!

Recently a story pertaining to this appeared in the news. In Florida, three children, aged 6, 4, and 1, were jumping on a trampoline. The mother of one of the children was supervising their play. Confident that the children were safe, she went inside the house. Upon returning a little later, she could not find the children. Worried, she called the police.

After a long search, the children were found in an old self-latching freezer near the trampoline. All of them had died of asphyxiation.

Check your house and yard now for any containers that have latches that cannot be opened from the inside!

Watch Those Stairs!

Every six minutes a child in the United States is taken to the emergency room because of a stair-related injury. Three out of four of these injured children will have head or neck injuries. One out of four was being carried by an adult.

One of the most common safety issues concerning stairs is pictured here. Although the hospital bill is, of course, theoretical, someone coming down the stairs and stepping on the debris could well crack his head as he slips. In a worst-case scenario, it could be worse than a trip to the hospital—it could be a trip to the morgue!

The lesson: *NEVER put things on stair steps, even temporarily.*

Can you find another safety issue in this photo? That's right—there is no handrail. The picture does not show the other side, so maybe the rail is there. However, if there is only one handrail (one on both sides is best) then it is ideally located on the right side when a person is descending, because most people are right-handed. And usually people get hurt while descending the stairs rather than ascending.

Do you see the hospital bill in this picture?

Get into the habit of using the handrail—even if you are young and think you don't need it! There is, after all, a secondary reason for always using the handrail—it slows people down! A handrail is like a sign saying, "SLOW DOWN!" We all know that accidents are more likely to happen when we are going too fast. The habit of using the railing will subconsciously slow us down.

There is also a third safety issue in the stairway picture. Can you find it? The issue is the dark areas. The light is coming from the wrong direction, creating dark areas on the steps. In this case, the light is from a window, so its position cannot be helped. However, all stairways should have a light that shines *into* the steps so that the user can clearly see the steps and any clutter that may be on them.

A word on tread size

The average man's shoe length is 11-12 inches. A study in Ireland found that with a tread depth on stairs of 10 inches, an overstep occurred an average of once every 10 *days*. On the other hand, with a tread depth of 12 inches, an overstep occurred only once every 73 *years*.

Modern building codes in the United States require a large tread size, but some areas do not have codes. And sometimes the codes are ignored, or the building was constructed before the codes were written. While you may not be able to replace an old stairway with narrow treads, keep adequate tread depth in mind when you are building that new deck or remodeling the house.

Notice the difference in how the curve of a shoe—which is the ball of the foot—fits on different tread depths. The ball of the foot should firmly land on the tread for a safe descent of the stairs.

Snow, ice, and water

During inclement weather we should be extra careful when using our outdoor stairways. While ice and snow obviously make ascending and descending more dangerous, even rain—or the lawn sprinkler—can cause steps to become slippery. With our arms loaded with groceries, we can easily forget that the steps are slicker than normal. And once inside, it is even easier to forget that while the stairs themselves are dry, your shoe soles are still wet! Speaking of carrying a load of groceries, never use a stairway unless you can keep one hand free for the railing. This is doubly true when carrying a child. Remember that one out of four stairway injuries among children occur when the child is being carried.

Stairway gates

Stairway gates are recommended both at the top and the bottom of the stairs in homes where small children live. These should remain in place until the child is old enough to safely maneuver the stairs by himself. Remember, once every six minutes a child arrives at an emergency room door because of a stairway accident. Don't let your child become a part of that statistic.

A Little Boy . . . on a Little Mower

The quiet of the August evening was broken by the hum of the five-horsepower Ariens mower as it slid back and forth across the lawn. Seven-year-old Merle was enjoying his job of keeping the grass under control while his siblings watched from a nearby window.

As he made a run across the yard, he noticed a stick lying in the mower's path. Fearing the blade would throw it through the window, he reached down to grab the stick and throw it out of the way. As Merle leaned forward, he suddenly slipped all the way off the mower. His hand on the steering wheel turned the mower toward him as he tumbled forward . . . right into the path of the freshly sharpened blades.

What happened next is almost too gruesome to tell, but the short form of the story is that Merle ended up grabbing the front of the mower as the deck came up over his lower body, chewing his legs as it came. Merle was dragged a few feet in this position—hanging on ferociously to the front of the mower—until his head hit the edge of the sidewalk, causing the mower to stall.

His family heard his cries for help and were soon at the scene. While Dad unwound Merle's pants and shredded leg from the mower blades, Mom called 911. Medics soon arrived, but several of them were so nauseated by the scene that they had to throw up. Blood was spraying everywhere, and Merle's leg was barely attached to his body—only by a narrow strip of skin. A helicopter ride and a two-week stay in the hospital followed, with emotional and physical ups and downs. Tears, long nights, operations, and anxious thoughts filled the following days. In what the doctors called a miracle, Merle survived the accident. His leg was successfully reattached to his body, and today he has only occasional pain. He lives a normal life, with a wife and several children.

A little boy, a little mistake—and a little too late to realize that little boys do not belong on riding lawnmowers. Even little five-horsepower ones!

Lawnmower safety review

With 9,000 children in the United States ending up in the emergency room every year from lawnmower accidents, a review of some safety issues seems warranted. Remember, these 9,000 are just the *children* who are injured. It does not include adults. Nor does it include children who received less serious injuries and were not taken to the hospital. Following is a list of lawnmower safety rules to keep in mind:

- Make sure a child is physically, emotionally, and mentally capable of handling power equipment before letting him or her operate a lawnmower. Just because a young boy can turn the steering wheel and put it in drive does not mean he is ready to mow the lawn.

- Keep other people away while mowing so they can't be hit by flying debris. Objects thrown by lawnmowers can be deadly. A piece of rock or a stick the size of a marble (or even smaller) coming out of the mower could permanently blind someone. It is best to search the lawn and pick up any debris before starting with the mowing. Otherwise, the temptation may be to stay on the mower and just lean over to pick up the debris, rather than shutting off the mower.

> Did you know that an object thrown from a power mower can fly at 200 mph and up to 50 feet?

- *No riders! Never!* Teach your children that a lawnmower is not a toy.

- Always wear good shoes when mowing. These protect the feet from any flying debris and provide more protection in the terrible event of the operator getting his foot into the blades.

- Always turn off the mower while crossing graveled lanes or paths.

- Use extreme caution when mowing on slopes. Do not let new operators mow slopes until they have learned to manage well on flatter areas. With

- riding mowers, it is best to mow up and down the hill. With push mowers, it is best to mow across the slope.

- Keep all safety guards and shields in place, and do not remove safety mechanisms on seats, clutches, and PTOs. They were put there for a reason.

- Always shut off the engine to unclog a mower. I have personally witnessed a child trying to unclog a mower with the engine running—and the blades still in gear! Such a child is not mature enough to operate power equipment.

- Avoid mowing wet grass; the extra slipperiness may cause the operator to fall or the machine to slide.

- Wear hearing protection while mowing.

- Shut off the engine to refuel, and always refuel outdoors, not in a garage or other building.

No Treats, Please!

Have you noticed a new trend among UPS, FedEx, and mail delivery drivers, as well as utility meter readers? If you do not have a dog running loose, as we do for varmint deterrence, you may not have noticed it.

Whenever the delivery drivers make a stop at our place, it has become almost standard procedure to give the dog a doggy biscuit. A few of the drivers actually seem to admire the dog, but most of them are mainly protecting their own skin—quite literally in some cases. They are operating on the old saying: "The best way to lose an enemy is to make him your friend." They know that if they give the dog a treat when they arrive, the dog will be less likely to chase them back to their vehicle—or worse. More than one delivery driver has asked me—from *inside* the vehicle, "Is the dog nice?"

There is a negative side to this. Once dogs have received treats when a big brown delivery truck pulls in, you can be sure they will come running every time it appears. If there was never a treat, the dogs would likely figure out that it is not worth the effort to get up from their afternoon nap.

How does this apply to safety? Some milk truck drivers, salesmen, and mail delivery people may also be in the habit of giving candy to children when they arrive. They probably mean no harm, and they certainly are not trying to protect themselves from an attack. They are simply trying to make a positive impression on the children or making an effort to express love toward them.

See what that man gave me!

The negative side to this is the same as with the dogs. If the children get a treat from the UPS driver every time he shows up, guess what happens? They always go running for the UPS truck when it appears! This creates a safety hazard because now the children are always around when the truck comes. So remain alert. Are all the children in a safe place when the driver is leaving? Or are the little ones perhaps standing behind the truck enjoying the treat—unseen by the driver?

For safety reasons, politely ask any candy-dispensing delivery drivers to refrain from passing out treats to your children. If you explain why, they will most likely understand without any offense.

Some families have a special spot where all the children are to gather (if they are playing in the yard) whenever a vehicle comes in the lane. This reinforces the idea that they are to avoid traffic.

Whether you decide to designate such a spot or not, teach your children to go *away* from traffic, not run toward it. The giving out of treats can subtly teach children the exact opposite.

Keep Medicines Up and Away!

About once every nine minutes a child in the United States is taken to an emergency room because of swallowing medicine that was not intended for the child. In one year's time, that is around 60,000 precious little children. How many others got into the medicine but were not taken in for examination?

We all know that small children tend to pop into their mouths whatever they happen upon. Also, many pills look similar to candy, so you have a double incentive to swallow something that could cause permanent damage or even kill them.

> A survey found that 9 out of 10 parents knew that medicines should be put up and away, but only 3 out of 10 actually did so.

Obviously, the first safety rule for medicines is to store them *up and away,* out of the children's reach and sight. Although many medicines have safety caps, some children still manage to get them open. Do not rely on the cap alone; consider it only a backup to the aforementioned guideline: *Always store medicines up and away.* And get into the habit of putting the cap back on medicine bottles as soon as you have taken out what you need.

Do you carry medicine in your purse or coat pocket? Make sure when you arrive at a guest's house or a church meeting that the medicine is not readily available to curious children. One child from a well-respected family sometimes secretly checked visitors' cars in hopes of finding candy or gum.

Some parents tell their children that their medicine is candy. Not only is that untrue, but in the child's mind it flattens the distinction between the two products. With that mindset, a child who does happen to get into the "candy" may just decide that ten pieces are better than one. Teach your children what medicine is for, and encourage them to take it bravely when needed. Don't try to make it "fun." Consider the consequences of always giving children medicines that taste like candy. Are you training the child that he should only do something if it gives him pleasure?

The American Association of Poison Control Centers has a 24-hour hotline available at 800-222-1222. Program the number into your phone or write it on your phone list.

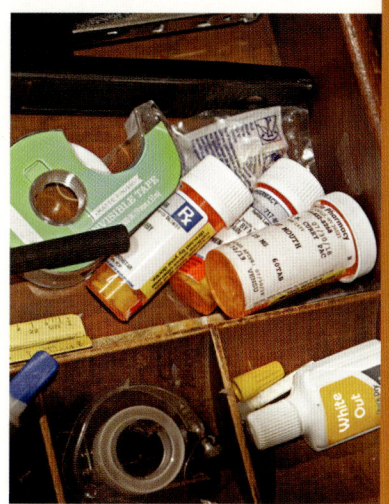

"Oh, there's Grandpa's candy that he eats every night before he goes to bed!"

Are Accidents God's Will?

The Bible reveals two seemingly contradictory truths. First, God is sovereign, meaning He is in control of everything and everyone. Nothing happens outside His control. 1 Chronicles 29:11-12 alludes to this in the following words:

> Thine, O LORD, is the greatness, and the power, and the glory, and the victory, and the majesty: for all that is in the heaven and in the earth is thine; thine is the kingdom, O LORD, and thou art exalted as head above all. Both riches and honour come of thee, and thou reignest over all; and in thine hand is power and might; and in thine hand it is to make great, and to give strength unto all.

On the other hand, humans have been given free will. God lets people make decisions and act upon those decisions without His interference. Deuteronomy 30:19 tells us:

> I call heaven and earth to record this day against you, that I have set before you life and death, blessing and cursing: therefore choose life, that both thou and thy seed may live.

Here we see that God offers people a chance to choose their own destiny. How does that mesh with God being in control of everything? Several illustrations can help us understand how these seeming contradictions work in perfect harmony.

We can think of a yard with a dog running loose. The owner lets the dog do whatever it wants, although he wants the dog to obey him. The owner sometimes intervenes, perhaps by stopping the dog from digging in the flowerbed or doing some other misdeed, but usually the dog is free to do as it pleases. The owner loves the dog and could put it in a small kennel where it would never get hurt and would always be safe. But because the owner genuinely cares about the dog, he wants it to have a better life than just sitting in a small kennel every day.

God *in a sense* relinquishes an aspect of His sovereignty by giving people the freedom to make their own decisions and allowing them to carry out those decisions, though I believe God can intervene at any time He chooses. This means that people are responsible for their decisions and actions in life. This is where the subject of sovereignty and free will touches the topic of safety.

"Well, it was just the will of God," people often say after an accident. But was it?

In 2 Peter 3:9 we read, "The Lord is not slack concerning his promise, as some men count slackness; but is longsuffering to us-ward, not willing that any should perish, but that all should come to repentance." Here we see an example of God allowing His will to be overruled by man's decisions. It is not God's will that people perish, yet millions upon millions have perished and are perishing. Is it the will of God that people fight, hate, and kill each other? No, that is not the will of God; yet God allows men to do those things.

I recently heard the true story of a young photographer who loved to climb to the top of tall buildings and take photos of himself sitting on the very edge, his feet dangling. He did this even when the buildings were locked, with no easy access to the roof. Somehow he found ways to get around these locked doors, perhaps by climbing out the window and scaling the last story, by crawling up through ventilation ducts, or by paying off the security guard.

About a year ago I heard the terrible news: this young man had fallen to his death while trying to make another daring photo. Was it "just the will of God" that this young man had died? Did God really want him to end his life as a splatter of bone and flesh on the street?

No, God's will was that this young man choose life, not death. It was God's will that he use his life for something more meaningful than taking pictures of himself in scary

Is it the will of God that this stunt photographer shows off?

situations. This young man made a tragic decision, and God did not intervene. When we make bad decisions that end up killing us—either physically or spiritually—we, not God, are responsible for our death.

Yet, in some cases, God does intervene in man's decisions and saves him from his own bad choices. Often the reason God intervenes in this way is because someone was praying. But that is a subject beyond the scope of this book.

Remember, God has set before us life and death. Don't choose death and then blame God when it happens. "It was just the will of God" should not be used to justify our lack of safety practices. Remember the young man who stepped out of God's will and fell from the top of a building while doing a foolish stunt!

Are There Exceptions to Safety Rules?

You can find pointed reminders in most safety bulletins and books, including this one, of things people should *always* do and things they should *never* do. For example, you may find a warning that reads, "Never stand on the top step of a stepladder."

How literally do we take that warning? Does that "never" mean absolutely never, as in "Never shoot yourself in the foot with a shotgun"? Or is it a relative thing, such as "Never point a nail gun at another person." Obviously, if the other person is 200 feet away, that "never" does not need to be regarded—unless the person is 200 feet *straight down!*

What about a safety rule that says, "Never try to walk on water"? That rule seems pretty obvious, but even that one could be disregarded if Jesus calls you out of a boat! So it seems that most safety rules do have some relativity about them, in varying degrees.

When can we stretch the "nevers" and the "always" and the "do nots"? We all know that we should "never" stand on the top step of a stepladder, right? But what if you only have about 30 seconds of painting left—just beyond what you can reach from the second step down of your stepladder? And reaching it safely according to normal safety procedures would mean going to town and spending $150 on another stepladder. Or perhaps spending an hour or two trying to find a neighbor to see if you could borrow a taller one. All you have to do is step up there to the top step, make a few swipes with the paintbrush for about 30 seconds, and you will be done.

Let's suppose you have something solid to hang on to, the ground is level and solid, and you will not be reaching outward. Or you might have someone to help stabilize the ladder while you make the finishing touches. In such a case, that "Never stand on the top step of a stepladder" can probably be safely ignored for the moment. (But please don't sue me if you fall off!)

The important principle for safety is to be mindful of what is totally safe, what is a little bit unsafe, what is really unsafe, and what is utter stupidity. A person who keeps these things in consideration can probably "bend the rules" occasionally and still do fine when he needs to get into the "little bit unsafe" territory. However, he will use wisdom and caution as he does so. For instance, he might have someone hold the stepladder while he stands on that top step for a few seconds. Or maybe he can find a way to tie a rope somewhere to have a handhold while he reaches up to paint with the other hand.

But someone who goes through life with a haughty "I do not need safety rules" attitude will be the one who takes foolish chances and will possibly pay dearly for it. He will clamber up to the top step of the stepladder, confident that "safety rules are for babies," and end up with a broken arm—or be in a casket.

To sum this up, *true safety is about principles, not specific rules.* However, we need the rules to help us understand the principles. Do not be afraid of safety rules, even if occasionally—with much caution and wisdom—you do bend them just a little!

Little Bad Batteries

"Hmm. Where did that little watch battery go? Must have gone under the chair. No big deal; it's just a tiny battery. I'll get another one."

No! It *is* a big deal! That little battery can cause big problems. Bad problems. Does having sixty surgeries, as one little boy experienced, sound like "no big deal"?

These tiny batteries, found in all kinds of gadgets these days, are capable of burning a hole in the esophagus within two hours if they lodge in a child's throat. It is the bigger batteries, about the size of a nickel, that cause the most problems. If the battery makes it all the way to the stomach, in most cases it does not cause health issues and just passes on through the digestive system.

Small but mighty!

Safety with little bad batteries

- Always find those dropped batteries and dispose of them properly so a child does not find them.

- Keep small batteries out of reach of children. It is preferable that small children do not even see the battery packs being opened, as they may think they are candy and later try to find them.

- Besides swallowing batteries, children have been known to put them into their ears or nose, which can also cause burns.

- Older people also need to be careful about swallowing batteries. This can happen when they reach for their pills on the nightstand and accidentally grab their hearing aid battery instead.

- Make sure the battery compartments on items are secured so small children cannot open them and get to the batteries. A screw-type cover is recommended. Consider putting a piece of tape over the cover as an extra precaution.

- Call the National Battery Ingestion Hotline at 800-498-8666 if you know or suspect that a child has swallowed a battery.

Kill Those Germs—Before They Kill You

Which do you think has killed more people, lions or mosquitoes? Of course, in this sense the little mosquito is more dangerous than the roaring lion. But even smaller than mosquitoes are the deadly germs, or better said, microbial life. Bacteria and viruses, unseen and unheard, kill or cripple millions of people every year.

Some of these tiny little killers can be in the food you eat. For this reason, a book about safety needs to address food preparation and storage. After all, if you manage to climb a ladder without falling off, what good does it do if you then swallow a bacterium that kills you? Do you realize that each year about 3,000 people in the United States die from food poisoning, while only about 300 die from falling off a ladder?

Three thousand may not seem like a huge amount compared to the tens of thousands that die from flu complications each year. But let's look at the entire world: 420,000 people die annually from food-borne illnesses. That means about 48 people per minute. Or in just over a second, another person will die of food poisoning somewhere in the world! About 1 out of every 10 people get sick each year from some kind of food poisoning.

Is it still a small matter to you? I hope not!

In the United States, government regulations have cut down on food-borne illnesses. Sometimes it seems that the government may be going overboard on their regulations. But on the flip side, we have one of the safest food supplies in the world. While the United States comprises over four percent of the world's population, we have less than one percent of the deaths from food poisoning. Have you thanked your government officials (and God) for that?

General rule of thumb

When it comes to killing a food-borne germ, the general rule of thumb is to beware of the temperature range between 40°F and 140°F. Below 40°F, practically all bacteria and viruses slow down their growth and become almost (but not entirely) incapable of harming people. However, we need to remember that while cold *disables* these germs, it does not necessarily *kill* them. That means that once the temperature warms back up above 40°, the germs can get back to their nasty work of making people sick.

At the other end of the scale, almost all food-borne germs are killed at a temperature above 140°F. While we were living in South America, we were able to keep soup from spoiling by boiling it for at least ten minutes every twenty-four hours. The boiling process killed all the bacteria, but since the soup was not kept cool, it was susceptible to airborne bacteria to reenter and multiply.

Canning safety

We have mentioned two methods of preserving foods: freezing and heating. There are others, but before moving on, let's review canning safety. We have seen the first principle behind canning—get the food hot enough to kill all the bad germs. However, unless the pasteurized food is stored to prevent reentry of airborne germs, it will soon become contaminated again. This is where canning comes in. If no air or liquid can contact the food that has been heated to kill the germs, it can be preserved for long periods of time.

With this in mind, we now understand why a canning jar must have a good seal. Detailed canning instructions are beyond the scope of this book, but we will review a few basic safety practices.

- Learn how hot each food must be heated to kill all the pathogens. Meats and non-acid foods require higher temperatures than high-acid foods. High acidity is an extra measure to guard against food poisoning since germs cannot live in highly acidic environments.

- Use good jars and lids, as a nick or a scratched lid may prevent it from sealing properly. While heating does kill germs, using clean jars and lids is common sense, as dirt may contain harmful bacteria.

- Keep your canner in shape with good seals and an accurate pressure gauge. Some state extension offices offer free pressure checks on canner pressure gauges.

- Check for a good seal 12 to 24 hours after removing the jars from the canner. The center of the lid should be sucked in. Do not store canned goods with the lid down. The bands/rings do not need to be left on the jar to maintain a good seal. They will tend to rust if left on, which may weaken the seal of the lid.

- Store canned goods in a dark, cool, dry location. The ideal temperature is 50 to 70°F.

- Bent-n-dent foods are often a good way to save money, but be careful with any cans that have a dented or bent rim because the seal may be broken. For that reason, some jurisdictions forbid selling any canned goods with a bent rim. I once bought a small can of crabmeat with a bent rim. When I opened it, the juice squirted all the way to the ceiling. It was obviously not fit for human consumption.

Preserving by drying

With the advent of pressure canning, our North American culture lost most of its knowledge about food preservation. While jerky is becoming a popular snack, at one time dried meat was the way most people kept meat.

This book is not about how to make jerky, but it is good to have a basic understanding of how it is preserved. Practically every living thing on earth needs water to survive, including humans and bacteria. So the safety principle behind drying for preservation is that if you remove all the water, all the germs die. Then, as long as the substance stays dry, no germs can take up residence again.

We made jerky in South America by taking beef and cutting it into slabs or strips about half an inch thick and hanging it over a clothesline for a day or two. To keep the flies off, we rubbed salt over the meat so the flies would not land and lay eggs. During the dry season, we could dry meat in only a day or two.

Foods other than meat can also be dried. The principle is the same. With no moisture, germs cannot survive. It is necessary to keep the flies away during the drying process, but screens or other methods can be used on foods you do not want to salt.

Acid preservation

Just as germs cannot survive in high heat or no moisture, they also cannot survive in high acid. Sauerkraut is preserved because no deadly germs can survive such a high acid content as vinegar. The truth of the matter is, if we humans had to live in a highly acidic surrounding, we would not survive long either.

While in South America, we also learned how to preserve a fish by soaking it in a vinegar mix. The vinegar "eats" at the bones, so after some weeks a bony fish can be eaten without any danger of getting a fishbone stuck in your throat. Meanwhile, the fish is preserved for many months without any cooking, canning, or refrigeration.

The same principle that keeps sauerkraut from spoiling also keeps wine from spoiling, except in this case alcohol is the preserving agent, not vinegar. For many centuries, turning some of the sugars in fruit juices into alcohol was the only truly efficient method known to preserve juices. Just as germs cannot live in high acids, they also cannot survive in high alcohol.

Obviously, the danger of preservation by alcohol is that while the alcohol does not kill a person drinking it, it does not take too much to make the person drunk. Today, thanks to the labors of Thomas Welch—who discovered and perfected the method for preserving grape juice without fermentation—we can have alcohol-free grape juice year-round.

Whether canning, pickling, or drying, simple safety measures can drastically reduce the possibility of becoming sick from food poisoning. Even if the only thing your safe food preservation practices do is keep you from upchucking your supper into the wastebasket, you will not regret taking the time to kill those germs!

Fun on the Ice

If I were to be paid my current hourly wage for every hour that I spent ice skating as a boy, I could . . . well, maybe take a nice long vacation somewhere. The wind could be howling and the temperature could be toward the bottom of the gauge, but somehow the lure of the ice would still draw us out. Only on rare occasions did we end up heading back to the house because it was too cold.

For all the hours we spent zipping around, it is a wonder none of us ended up cracking our heads or breaking an arm—or even twisting a knee. Somehow we never ended up among the 50,000 people in the United States who injure themselves each year while ice skating.[1]

The exhilaration of gliding over the ice after a long day at school!

Of course, we sometimes fell, and we knocked each other over in our homespun hockey games. The time I got the brainstorm to ride my bike on the ice was perhaps my worst incident. "I will just put my foot down if my wheels start to slip sideways," I wisely informed myself.

Yes, I did put my foot down when those wheels started slipping sideways. But by then it was too late to realize that my foot might also slip. I had not even made it to the swamp yet. I was only on a puddle in the lane when the foolishness of my idea was finally cracked into my brain. As far as I can remember, this was the only time I ever hit my head hard on the ice. And I never tried the bike-on-ice idea again!

But others have not been as blessed as I was. Concussions and traumatic brain injuries can happen easily while ice skating. A good knit cap or even a helmet should be considered essential safety gear, especially for those who are just learning to skate.

Most ice skates these days are high top, meaning they go over the ankle. For this reason, knee injuries may be more common than twisted ankles. The most common-sense ice-skating safety rule is probably as simple as knowing and acknowledging your level of ability while on skates. Let those who are more practiced zip around if they wish, but beginners should stay in the low-speed areas until they have mastered the techniques. As with most other accidents, the faster you are going, the more likely you are to injure yourself or others. But beyond this simple rule, make sure your skates fit well. Oversized skates mean less control with the ankle, leading to a greater danger of ankle sprains. Skates that are too tight will not give the ankle enough liberty to do its job.

Sharpen your skates at least once a season. But remember, anyone falling on those sharp edges can easily be cut. This warning is especially pertinent for hockey games where some jostling is normal.

Dress warmly! Wear layers, and be careful about working up a sweat and then having to deal with getting chilled. If you have to walk home, prepare for it. Growing up on our home farm, we walked home through the fields after skating, and it seemed the cold penetrated faster when we were walking than when we were skating. When the thermometer is at its lowest point (in northern climates), it may be best to stay inside. Frostbitten toes, cheeks, or fingers are not worth it.

Ice safety

Ice skating is just one area of ice safety. Ice fishers, hunters, trappers, and anyone out for a walk may encounter ice that they want to traverse. Our general rule for ice skating when I was a boy was that ice needed to be at least four inches thick. I did some quick research just now, and that seems to be a good rule. Two or three inches of ice may hold one person quite well, but what about four people in one spot? And what about variations in thickness? You may have found an area of ice that is three inches thick, but what if the rest of the ice only averages two inches?

Obviously, the depth of the water makes a difference as well. Most of our ice skating when I was young was on swampy areas or flooded parts of fields, where the water was around two feet deep at most. When we did skate over deeper water, we were more careful to make sure the ice was thick enough. While a person can drown in shallow water, the greater risk is getting excessively chilled by a breakthrough.

Following are some general recommendations for minimum ice thickness:

- Less than four inches — Stay off!
- Four inches — ice skating and other foot traffic.
- Five inches — Snowmobile or ATV
- Eight inches — Small car or pickup
- Twelve inches — Medium pickup

Again, remember that these figures are not for *groups*. In other words, do not park ten cars close together on eight inches of ice, unless you want those cars to look like a picture I saw recently in which half a dozen vehicles were falling through the ice. One recommendation when using a vehicle on ice is to drill a hole in the ice near the vehicle, and if water starts pushing up out of the ice you know the ice is starting to sink. Even if no water pushes up, move a parked vehicle every two hours to help prevent sinking. If it is evident that others have been parking their vehicles in a certain ice-fishing hotspot, find a new place for yours, as continual parking in one spot may weaken the ice.

Measure the ice approximately every 150 feet if you are moving to another location. Water currents can wear against the bottom of the ice and cause the ice to

become thinner in pockets of warm water, such as when a spring at the bottom of a lake or pond injects warmer water into an area. Even schools of fish stirring the water can affect ice thickness. If traveling on ice, such as with a snowmobile, wearing a life jacket will help keep you afloat if you do break through. Remember, falling into the water adds a lot of extra weight, which will make it much more difficult to climb out of the water and back onto firm ice. For this reason, it is good to carry some type of ice pick or claw in your pocket to help "dig" yourself back onto the ice in the event of a breakthrough.

Know the different types of ice. Fresh, clear ice is twice as strong as white ice, which may be snow that has half melted and then frozen again. Older clear ice is not as strong as fresh ice. Gray and white ice should always be considered untrustworthy. One saying goes:

Thick and blue,
Tried and true.
White and crispy,
Way too risky!

Water: Friend and Foe

When thinking of safety and ponds, my mind goes back to my childhood. I remember as a boy of about five years of age standing behind the barn on the farm in Indiana, watching a bulldozer build a dam across a gully. Talk about excitement!

Anybody who knows even the least bit about boys and water puddles know that a sort of magnetic attraction exists between the two. And now Dad was having a half-acre "puddle" built. When the dam was finished, gravel was laid at the shallow end for a wading spot, and the water began to build up. Soon it was full, probably eight to ten feet deep at the deepest end, sloping off to

Ah, the joys of fishing on a farm pond!

around three feet deep at the wading end.

Over the next few years, I grew bigger but never really learned to swim well. I stayed at the shallow end, splashing around while trying to swim and learning to float. Any family who knows the pleasure of swimming on a hot summer afternoon can relate to what I am talking about.

Meanwhile, Dad and my older brothers and their friends were in the deeper water. They often swung out over the water with a rope hanging from a branch of a big tree Dad had left growing at the water's edge. It looked like one of the greatest thrills a boy could experience—to run down the bank, swing out over the water, and let go with a plunge.

Of course, I never dared to try it. I was scared of water, which was probably a good thing. Dad set down a basic rule for us: those who could not swim were not to swing on the rope unless he was there in the water to help us if we fell in. I cannot say that I remember now that I ever heard Dad specifically say those words, but I knew it was one of his rules.

How did I know? Well, one day our cousins showed up. I was about eight years old by then, and my older sisters were about ten and twelve. I didn't have a cousin my age, so I trudged along behind my sisters as they showed our cousins around the farm. They probably felt like I was a little nuisance, but it was exciting for me.

Of course, we ended up looking at the pond, and I suddenly had the idea that this would be the time to impress everyone. "Watch me swing out over the water!" I cried. I grabbed the rope, made the run, swung out over the water, and landed safely back on the bank.

But my time of glorying was short-lived. My oldest sister exclaimed, "I'm telling Dad!" And off the girls headed for the house, two hundred yards away.

My little heart knew what that meant. I saw some tall "horse weeds" growing nearby and decided I would play in them for a while. Of course, I would never have admitted to myself that I was hiding from Dad and was hoping he would just forget about the incident. Sometimes our little minds have funny ideas!

Bless Dad! He did what a good father should do, and it was only about ten minutes later that he found me in the weeds, "playing." He administered the appropriate discipline, which some people today might call child abuse. My dad is no longer living, but I will bless him publicly once again. He took time out of his busy day to walk the two hundred yards to where I was and administer the needed correction. I never swung out on the rope again, except possibly when he was there in the water.

As I think of that story now, with tears of gratitude for my father's actions, another aspect needs to be considered. We children were for the most part obedient and respectful to Dad and Mom. But as is normal, we all had our Proverbs 22:15 moments: "Foolishness is bound in the heart of a child, but the rod of correction shall drive it far from him."

What boy would not be tempted with this sight?

My point is that we need to make safety applications even if our children are obedient and respectful. The pull of water—and showing off—is sometimes just too great for boys to resist. I was well aware of Dad's rule: "Don't swing on that rope over the pond." But obedient and respectful as I was, I still fell for the temptation.

What are some of the recommended safety precautions for ponds? First of all, ponds should be fenced off if possible. Of course, a disobedient child can always climb a fence, but imagine how much safer I would have been if my sister would have warned me as soon as I started climbing the fence. If a pond cannot be fenced, or the family cannot afford to do so, then the rope should be out of reach of the smaller children. I do not wish to be too harsh on my dad for not taking these extra precautions, but they are good recommendations.

Statistics indicate that most drowning victims in farm ponds are under the age of four, and they often drown in the shallow edges of the pond after slipping in while playing near the edge. After birth defects, drowning is the leading cause of death for children under four years of age in the United States.[2] This is where a fence around the pool or pond comes in. A fence may not stop an older child from finding a way over it, but it is less likely that smaller children will try to circumvent it.

When swimming, a rope, a pole, and a life buoy should all be readily available. The rope should be long enough to reach all the way across the pool or pond so two people can each grab an end and have the rope go completely across the water. Such a rope is safer than throwing one end out to a distressed swimmer.

No one should ever swim alone. I remember seeing my older brother suddenly get swimming cramps. My brother knew how to swim, but he was fortunate to be in shallow water when the cramps hit him. When you get cramps, you had better have someone available to help even if you are an excellent swimmer. For this and other safety reasons, no one should ever swim alone.

For those just learning to swim, one of the first things they should learn is how to float without a safety jacket. It is a simple maneuver, and when learned, it helps take away the dangerous fear of water that leads to panic. A panicked person is much more likely to drown than someone who is calm. Learning the simple technique of floating, which takes little physical effort in calm water, gives a person a sense of security. Once a person knows that the calmer waters are manageable, he is less likely to panic even in rough waters. This is not to advocate that those who know how to float should not wear safety jackets. However, learning the technique can greatly aid against panic and help in situations where someone ends up in deep water accidentally.

Don't even think about trying to outswim the thousands of pounds of water falling over these rocks every minute!

Never dive into water without checking for rocks or sticks that may be protruding from the bottom. This is doubly important in creeks and rivers, where objects can be washed into places that were suitable diving spots just the previous day.

Be careful about diving into water when you are overheated. I heard of a young man who died when he jumped into a cold creek on a hot day. The temperature shock was simply too great for his hot body, and the shock killed him almost instantly.

In general, we should be careful with cold water. A swimmer can lose a lot of body heat in cold water—and a cold swimmer is a weak swimmer.

Never swim when lightning is in the area. When lightning strikes a body of water, the electricity can spread throughout the whole pond or lake. Wait at least thirty minutes after the last lightning strike before entering the water.

Drink plenty of liquids before and during a long swim. Human skin is one of the most waterproof materials known to man, and even though you may be submerged in water, you are not absorbing water into your body. In fact, you may be losing water through the sweat glands and dehydrating. Of course, do not drink the pond or creek water; take some clean water along.

Beware of falling water. Even a small stream, if it is rushing along, can hold a good swimmer under water. A 55-gallon drum of water weighs 440 pounds. Picture yourself getting 440 pounds of water dropped on you. Then, about the time you recover, you are hit with another 440 pounds. This happens again and again. It's only a barrel of water, right? But if the barrels of water are continuous, you do not stand a chance of fighting back.

If you are thrown into rushing water, try to float with your feet downstream so you can occasionally raise your head to see where you are going. The U.S. Forest Service says that most people drown in streams and rivers when a foot or leg gets caught in a crevice or underwater tree branch and the water pulls them under the surface.

Rip currents

A rip current is when water in the ocean or a larger lake is blown to shore and then flows back out in a channel. In some areas, the bottom of the ocean or lake has a trough cut into it. When that is the case, the water that has blown to shore will flow back out more swiftly in that trough. This strong outward flow of water can carry a swimmer away from shore. In some situations, the flow of water going out is faster and stronger than even good swimmers

Can you see the rip current? A red flag marks this one.

45

can fight. A rip current does not pull people under the water, it simply carries them out faster than they can swim to shore. Rip currents are among the leading causes of drowning in larger bodies of water, as the victim wears out trying to swim against the current.

If caught in a rip current, swim at a 90° angle to the current, which would mean swimming parallel with the shore instead of toward the shore. Once you are out of the rip current, you can turn toward the shore. Another option is letting yourself float out a bit and then swimming to the side of the current before heading back toward the shore. What will *not* work is trying to outfight the current by swimming directly against it. Watch for signs of rip currents before entering the water at a beach. If you notice foam and floating objects flowing back out into deep water in a certain spot, it is likely because of a rip current.

Rescuing a drowning person

This subject is a hard one. Why? Because if you are watching a loved one drown, the natural reaction will be to enter the water to try to save the person. Yet, most safety organizations warn against trying to save a drowning person in deep water.

Drowning victims are usually in a panic and will try to climb on top of anyone who approaches to save them. Even good swimmers can have a hard time saving a panicked swimmer in deep water. And too many times there are then two drowning deaths instead of just one. Reaching out with a rope or a pole, or something like a life vest or inner tube, is much better than trying to swim out to a drowning person.

Of course, in some situations nothing is available to throw or take out to the drowning person. There are special techniques that lifeguards learn for rescuing a drowning person in deep water, but that is beyond the scope of this book. The important thing is to avoid getting into situations where drownings occur. How to discern when you should try to save a drowning person by entering the water and when you have to turn the situation over to God is also beyond what this book can teach you. Obviously, if a two-year-old child is drowning in three feet of water, even a non-swimming adult should enter the water to help. But if a 180-pound man is drowning in water ten feet deep, should a 120-pound woman who doesn't know how to swim jump in and try to pull him out? No.

One big misconception of drowning victims is that they will scream for help. Most people who are drowning are so busy fighting to stay above the water (often because of panic) that they cannot scream. Rather than waiting for a cry for help, watch for signs of struggling swimmers. Most people who drown do *not* scream or holler for help. An instinct in drowning people is to throw their heads back and open their mouths wide, gasping for air. They are so busy gasping for air that they cannot call for help.

Always keep in mind that rescuing a drowning swimmer in deep water is very difficult without special training. Also, if someone has been pulled out of the water in a near-drowning incident, be aware that small amounts of water in the lungs can cause death several hours later. This is known as *secondary drowning*. Coughing and sputtering because of sucking in a little water is normal, but rescuers should watch for signs of continued coughing and sputtering for several hours after the rescue.

A similar situation is called *dry drowning*. This occurs when water is sucked in but does not go all the way to the lungs. The vocal cords then start going into spasms, cutting off the airways. This can lead to death, even though the person has been out of the water for an hour or more.

Hopefully, none of us ever has to make the hard decision for rescue situations that are risky or beyond our capabilities. The important safety rule for water is the same as for other dangers: *Avoid dangerous situations in the first place.* This will save us from having to deal with accidents because of our failure to practice common sense.

Batter Up . . . Pitcher Down!

Carefully 15-year-old Gary prepared to pitch the ball. There was one out and one runner on base.

The youth and their parents were enjoying their annual fall picnic. After a tasty lunch, a friendly softball game was now underway. It was only the third inning and the score was close.

Even the weather was cooperating. It was a perfect September day—warm, but not too warm. Just right for playing ball! For the older folks, it was a time to relax and visit—and to watch the action on the ballfield.

Gary's older brother Phil was up to bat. As Gary pitched the ball, Phil tensed for

the strike. Here it came . . . a nice pitch. *Whack!* A second later there was another *whack* as Gary tried, but failed, to get his glove up in time. With a sickening thud, the ball hit him in the head, and he slumped to the ground.

Instantly the atmosphere changed. The ballgame was forgotten and the visiting came to a sudden halt as people rushed to the scene. Phil, his heart in turmoil, was one of the first to be there, with his parents not far behind.

As Gary lay quietly on the ground, no one knew what to expect. Was he seriously hurt—or even killed? While someone called 911, others worked on reviving Gary and evaluating him. Everyone breathed a sigh of relief when after a few minutes he started responding. It also soon became apparent that the ball had struck him on the side of the face, making a brain injury less likely.

Gary was fortunate. He ended up with no major issues except several broken teeth, for which he would have to see a dentist. Gary and his family—and perhaps most of all Phil—are thankful to God for His protecting hand. What could have been a tragedy was only a reminder of the uncertainty of life.

Keeping the game safe and enjoyable

I think most of us have seen situations like this. Softball is a popular game, both in schools and at social events like reunions and picnics. People enjoy it because it takes skill and teamwork. And in schools, especially, it teaches good sportsmanship.

However, because of its very nature, softball is a somewhat dangerous game. Think of it; we take a solid bat and hit a fairly solid ball as hard as possible. A hard line drive can be traveling at 70 mph or more—as can a hard throw. All is fine as long as the ball lands in a player's glove. But when someone gets hit, serious injuries can result.

What are some ways we can minimize the danger? Let's consider some basic softball recommendations for a safe and enjoyable game.

- Softballs are rated by their COR value. This refers to the tension, or bounce, of the ball. When a softball with a COR value of .50 is thrown against a wall at 80 mph, it will bounce back at 40 mph. The top-rated softballs with a normal 12" circumference are .47 COR, such as the well-known Blue Dot. These balls have a lot of bounce, and players like them. They can be dangerous, however, especially when used in social settings. One step down is the .44 COR ball, like the Gold Dot. This is a much better choice. Yes, it is 6% slower, but that is a small price to pay for making the game safer. The smaller 11" balls, such as Green Dot, should also be avoided. *Stick with a standard size .44 COR ball in all social ballgames!*

- The pitcher has the most dangerous position. Two basic rules can help avoid injuries.

    » *The pitcher must be a good player and be able to move quickly.* When men or youth boys are playing, the pitcher can face fierce line drives, so it is not wise to put in a girl or younger boy as pitcher.

    » *Stand back at least 45 feet to pitch.* This may make pitching a bit more difficult, but those extra few feet make a big difference in situations such as Gary's.

- Use common sense when throwing the ball. *If it's too late to get the runner out by throwing sensibly—DON'T THROW!* It is these frantic, last-second throws that often hurt someone.

- Use extra care when trying to throw out a runner at home. Remember that the runner has his back turned and will not see the ball coming. Wild throws—sometimes coming from the outfield!—are dangerous. I remember a young boy at a school picnic who peeped around the backstop just as one of these wild throws came in. It hit him right on the side of the head. The lesson is clear: *Look and think before you throw.*

- Spectators should stay behind the backstop or somewhere else out of the line of fire. Close to first base is not a good place to sit!

- And finally, remember that it's just a game. Safety is more important than winning.

Kidnapping—Mom's Greatest Fear

Every mother has her own greatest fear concerning her children's safety, but the fear of her child being randomly stolen or abducted surely ranks near the top. Statistically speaking, however, that fear should rank near the bottom in the United States because the random abduction of a child only happens about once a day. While that may seem like a lot—and indeed even once a year would be horrible enough—it is relatively low if you compare that number to some of the other statistics in this book.

So why all the missing children posters? If you notice the wording in the above paragraph, it says *randomly* stolen or abducted. Less than 1 percent of all missing children reported in the United States involve a stranger luring or grabbing a child. Over 90 percent of these reported missing children are runaways, most of them teenagers.[3] In other words, they are older teens who for whatever reason have decided to leave home without their parents' consent. About 5 percent of the children reported missing in the United States are family abduction cases. This means that another member of the family has taken the child, most likely in a divorce custody situation where one parent steals the child from the other parent.

This safety book is not geared toward helping parents relate to their children, which is the underlying cause of 90 percent of missing children who run away from home. If you are a parent struggling to relate to your child, seek some help and guidance, both from God and from a community of believers. If you are a teen who is struggling to relate to your parents, the same advice applies. Just be aware, dear struggling teen, that most of the children who run away from home end up in situations that are worse—many times worse—than their original home life. Seek some help from a stable adult if you are struggling in your home life. You will be much better off trying to make the best of the situation rather than running away to a friend's house or living on the street, where many people are out to take advantage of vulnerable runaways.

To stop a kidnapper

Although kidnapping and random abduction of children are both relatively rare in the United States, it does happen, and it has happened even in our rural Plain communities. The recent random abduction of two Amish children from their family's produce stand in New York comes to mind.[4] What can be done to deter these situations?

First of all, although it is not good to go through life with a "kidnapper lurking behind every bush" mentality, be aware that kidnapping does happen. Do not let children run a produce stand by themselves, especially if it is located away from the house. Abductors usually study and prepare for their kidnapping, choosing situations and times when it is easier to pull off their evil deed. By planning ahead and being careful, you can do much to discourage an abduction.

The majority of child abductions are of school-aged children, not preschoolers. This is because preschoolers tend to stay closer to their parents, while school-aged children are more likely to walk to school and be playing by themselves or with a small group of other children. Going to and from school are the most likely times to be abducted, since kidnappers usually study their victims and watch for a routine. Tending a produce stand or other place of business is also a routine that abductors might consider an opportunity to snatch a child.

While teaching children to respect strangers, we also need to teach them to say no to offers of free candy, rides, or money. The abductor may also offer to show the child an interesting picture or give the opportunity

Abductors sometimes lure children into vehicles with candy or the promise to see an animal or other interesting object. "Would you like to pet my big kitty on the back seat?" they may say. Hopefully you have trained your child to say, "No thanks!"

51

to look at or pet an animal. These are potential ways to lure a child into a car. For older girls, the abductor may lure them by showering them with special attention that will play on the girl's feminine emotions.

In some cases, abductors will simply use force, or the threat of force, perhaps by displaying a gun or knife. Teach your children to scream if they feel threatened. Screaming is a major deterrent, since attention is the last thing the abductor wants. Of course, teaching your children to pray should also be at the top of the list of safety measures.

Away from home

A mother losing track of a child in a store is one of those things that will likely happen to most families. Even Jesus' parents lost track of Him during a festival. Most of the time it is a simple matter of looking in the adjoining aisle or two. Perhaps for older children, it may mean a trip to the toy section of the store.

Despite the fear of someone nabbing a child in a store—and we hear stories of it occasionally—remember that it does not happen often. Just think what it would take to pull off a successful kidnapping in a public store, and you will soon realize it would be no easy task. Most kidnappers are smart enough to realize that. However, when people are drunk, depressed, or angry, they may do things they normally would not do. So we need to use wisdom and caution.

You would never, ever put up a sign like I did here. But is your produce stand or business managed and arranged in such a way that a predator could easily think this?

What are some simple precautions? Train older children to stay by your side, even if the boys have to wait for fifteen minutes in the material section while Mom chooses dress fabric or waits for it to be cut. When I was a boy, Mom gave us permission to wait for her in the toy section of Farm and Fleet, and she could always find us there, gaping at the new tractors and trucks on the shelves. Due to the changing dynamics of the toy section, and the slightly higher chance of an abduction, that should no longer be an option in today's cultural climate.

Be careful around rest stops while on long-distance trips, especially in isolated areas at night. Public bathrooms at bus or train stations are another place you do not want to let your children enter unattended. Again, teach your children to refuse random gifts of candy from strangers in these areas unless you are overseeing the situation. Teach them never to follow a stranger who may tell them, "Your daddy sent me here to take you to him."

With these simple guidelines, we should be able to avoid most of the situations that would invite a stranger to abduct one of our children. In foreign countries, the situation may be many times worse, and closer oversight of our children will be necessary. The rule is still pretty simple: think like a kidnapper, and avoid places and situations that would make it easy to grab or entice your child.

Fire Safety

Scorched Kitchen for Breakfast

Joel poured one-half inch of corn oil into the frying pan. To get things moving for the morning school rush, he set the electric stove on 9, the maximum setting, and left the room temporarily. He knew better than to try to cook at that temperature, but he planned to lower the burner to 4 in a minute.

Getting the children ready for school is a good time to forget things like burners turned too high. Joel doesn't remember what it was that made him forget. He does remember the scream that came resounding through the house a short time later: "Fire!"

"Papa, it's burning!" Marcia cried out.

"Okay, just lower it," Joel ordered.

Marcia once again told her father, who was in another part of the house, "It's burning!"

"Okay, so what? Just turn it down."

"I can't!" she replied loudly.

Joel thought his daughter was just too busy to watch what she was cooking. To him, "burning" meant she was burning something like a piece of toast. He wondered why she didn't just turn it down so it wouldn't burn. He hollered into the kitchen again, "Okay, just turn it off completely."

"I can't!" came the reply. Joel was confused. The voice of his daughter was loud but not panicky.

Entering the kitchen, he found the oil burning, sending flames to the nearby microwave and the cabinets above.

"Why didn't you tell me it was on fire?" he quickly asked.

"I did!" Marcia replied.

Joel sent his boys to get the fire extinguisher from the wall in another room. His mind raced. *What should I do?*

"We can't get the fire extinguisher off!" the boys cried out.

"Just pull it!" Joel shouted back.

Joel knew better than to pour water over the burning oil. The water would turn to steam immediately when hitting the hot oil and cause it to spray in all directions. By now the flames were leaping up to the ceiling. Grabbing the frying pan, Joel took it to the sink and poured the oil down the drain, then turned the water onto the skillet. Burning droplets of oil sprayed in every direction, but they did not burn long.

The scorched microwave.

Although the fire was out, the hot oil that had splattered everywhere began to smoke terribly. For a few minutes it was so dense that Joel and his family could not see through it, and it was hot enough to kick on the microwave fan.

Opening all the doors and windows soon cleared out the smoke. The ceiling had some smoke damage and the microwave was scorched, but other than some shaken emotions, no one was injured.

Lessons

What did Joel learn that morning? He says the following points were lessons from the incident:

- "I never knew it is so easy to start a grease fire. Never leave a frying pan on maximum heat!" Fire experts say a pan of hot oil can burst into flames on a hot burner in as little as thirty seconds.

- "I would have only had to cover the fire to put it out." This smothering method is by far the best option. Pouring water on a grease fire is *never* recommended.

- "Now my fire alarm is working."
- "If the fire had spread, we could have been minutes from losing our entire house." Once wood heats up, it lets off flammable gases that can burn before the wood itself actually does.
- "I hope someone else can learn a lesson from this and save their home and possibly their life."
- "God is merciful. We have no insurance on our home."

Twenty-three years earlier, Joel had seen a friend drop a frozen chicken into hot oil. The oil spewed out of the pan like a spray bottle because of the water vaporizing in the heat and "blowing" the oil about. As the oil started burning from the flames of the gas stove, the man grabbed the pan and ran around in circles before finally throwing it out the door.

If you find a grease fire on your stove, the following are recommendations by fire experts. Only try these if the fire is small.

- Turn off the burner. That is step one!
- The best method to extinguish the flames is to cover the fire with a lid or a cookie sheet. This will only work, of course, if the flames are limited to the oil inside the pan.
- Baking soda and salt can be used to smother small grease fires. Do not use flour, baking powder, or sugar, as these can burn.
- A Class B dry chemical fire extinguisher can be used on grease fires.
- Do not use water, as this can cause the grease to splatter everywhere.
- Call 911 immediately if the fire is not quickly responsive to your efforts.

Each year 160,000 home fires occur in the United States, with two-thirds of these being cooking fires. Cooking fires are the number one cause of house fires. Yes, it can happen to you!

This grease fire test shows what happens when water is poured on a grease fire.

Don't Burn the House with the Hotdogs!

Each year they cause 7,000 injuries and 10,000 home fires in the United States. What are they?

Grills!

Most of the injuries are likely minor burns, but with U.S. fire departments responding to an average of nearly one home fire related to a grill every hour, this is no minor matter.

Grilling safety is mostly a matter of forethought. If we consider how a grill fire could get out of hand, several safety practices should pop into our minds.

First, keep the grill at least ten feet away from the house or other outbuildings. Of those 10,000 grill-related annual home fires mentioned in the first paragraph, more than 2,500 were on a balcony, porch, patio, terrace, or courtyard. In other words, the grill was not *in* the house, but it was in or on a structure *connected* to the house. Obviously, grills are not designed to be used inside a structure, but it is easy to assume that as long as the grill is outside the main house, that is all that matters.

When we think of grilling, we usually think first of savory steaks and barbecued hamburgers. The problem is that the very thing that makes the meat so tasty is what makes grilling so fire-prone: fat.

Fats are very flammable, which is why flare-ups are common while grilling meats. For this reason, never use a grill where limbs or hanging items are above the grill. Picture a beautiful oak tree in the late fall, with its leaves brown but still hanging on the branches. Then picture a flare-up from a grill setting an overhanging limb on fire . . . with the flames rapidly spreading through the whole tree. Or consider dried flowers hanging from the ceiling of a porch, with a flare-up from the grill lighting them like a fuse!

The tasty fats from those juicy steaks can also heat up and flow out from the bottom of the grill, then catch on fire. For this reason, grills should never be loaded to the max with meats. While cooking, it is safer to have the lid closed to contain any flare-ups from burning fat as it drips out of the meat.

This rubber hose does not currently leak, but how long before it will?

If your grill is gas-fired, be sure to check the rubber hoses annually for cracks. One method to discover a leaky hose is to cover the hose with soapy water and then turn on the gas; any leaks in the line will cause bubbles in the soapy water. It may seem unnecessary to say so, but do not turn on the gas with the lid closed to light the grill!

For charcoal grills, make sure the metal on the bottom of the grill is not rusted thin. Clean out the ashes regularly. And definitely do not let them sit in the grill over winter or for extended periods of time. Ashes can hold moisture and create hidden rust issues. When the metal rusts thin enough, a bump or jar can cause it to suddenly fail and let hot coals dump out the bottom.

This grill burner needs major repair before use. Or more likely a replacement!

When grilling, do not wear loose-fitting or flowing clothes, and watch for shirttails and apron strings that can inadvertently get into the open flames. Keep a fire extinguisher or water hose handy while grilling.

Speaking of grilling, may I order a barbecued pork chop?

Firing Up the Old Wood Stove

If you have ever done an internet search for "wood stove safety," you will quickly see that some of the top results are from insurance companies. Suffice it to say that insurance companies and wood stoves get along like sworn enemies!

There is a reason for this cold hatred. Wood stoves cause so many home fires that insurance companies are loath to insure a house with a fireplace or wood-burning stove, especially in rental houses. Some simply refuse to consider offering insurance until the stove or fireplace is removed or dismantled.

One of the reasons for increased home fires from wood stoves and fireplaces is that a generation or two has grown up without using wood as a home heat source. Imagine my surprise—and amusement—when I went camping as a young man with a couple of other farm boys. When it came time to light the fire, one of the teenaged boys took a match and tried to light a large chunk of firewood with it. One would think a farm boy should know better than that!

Now imagine how much less people who grow up in urban areas know about heating with wood. They don't even have to burn the trash—it is all disposed of elsewhere. Placing these people in a home with a wood stove is an invitation for trouble.

Wood stove safety, like other safety categories, is a matter of using some good old common sense. An older single man I knew moved into a cabin and set up a wood stove. The problem was that he put the stove right on the wooden floor, with no legs or spacing. He lit the stove and then went to sleep.

Thankfully, he survived the disaster that followed. Ever since I have wondered why an old man with a white beard would do such a thing as place a wood-burning stove directly on a wooden floor!

Don't even think about doing it!

Then there is the use of combustible liquids like gasoline and kerosene to start a fire. I know how frustrating it can be. The fire has died out overnight, the house is cold, and the kindling is gone. The solution seems simple—use a little kerosene, diesel fuel, or gasoline to get the morning off to cozy start.

Don't do it! Don't even think about doing it! How many houses will have to burn down, how many hospital bills for burned arms and faces will we have to pay, before a very simple rule sinks in? *Never put combustible liquids on a fire that has died out!*

My own family history also has a fire safety story. My dad and two older brothers were burning brush one day. The boys, about ten and twelve years old, were trying to get the brush pile to burn while Dad was plowing or doing something on the tractor in the same field. When Ray couldn't get the pile to ignite, he finally climbed on top of the pile and began pouring gasoline all over it.

Imagine my father on the other side of the field on the tractor watching this. He frantically tried to get Ray's attention. What if there was even one little spark of fire still active from his previous attempts to light the pile? But there he was, right on top, pouring gas over the whole pile in frustration.

Don't even think about it!

Thankfully the pile did not ignite, and Dad was able to give Ray a safety lecture when he finally got his attention. But others have not always been so fortunate. Too many stories like this have ended with serious burns or explosions as some lingering spark ignited the fuel. In more than one instance, someone splashed a little kerosene onto a small fire only to find out too late that the container held gasoline. This can have devastating consequences.

Don't do it! Take a few minutes to find some old newspaper or make a few kindling pieces with a hatchet to start that morning fire. Yes, it is slower—but much safer.

More wood burning safety

- Fire safety officials in the United States recommend covering any combustible material within 36 inches of a wood stove with a piece of sheet metal spaced one inch in front of the material. This spacing is to allow for air ventilation behind the metal. If the metal (or even bricks and rock) come into direct contact with the combustible material, the heat buildup can still create a fire. Even thick rock material can eventually build up enough heat to transfer to the combustible material.

- A metal floor protector should extend at least 18 inches beyond the edge of the stove, with 24 inches to the front. This should be on top of bricks or rock material, especially if the stove sits less than 6 inches off a combustible floor.

- If a stovepipe runs through a combustible wall or ceiling, remove all combustible materials within 18 inches, with the exception of an approved insulated chimney thimble. With a thimble, only 12 inches of clearance is required.

- Never connect more than one stove or fireplace to a chimney.

- Never connect another type of vent (such as a gas water heater) into a chimney used for a fireplace or woodstove.

- Always inspect chimneys in old houses before using them for wood stoves.
- Most of the chimneys built before 1950 are not lined, and even in newer houses linings may be damaged.
- Burning green wood causes creosote buildup, which is the source of chimney fires. Any creosote thicker than one-fourth inch is potential fuel for a chimney fire.
- A short, hot fire is better than a long, smoky one to prevent creosote buildup. Cool chimneys will promote the creation of creosote.
- Always empty ashes into a sealed metal container. Yes, people have been known to put their ashes into the kitchen trash can—with a fire as a result!

House Fires: Dark, Quick, and Deadly

Although it may seem strange, a house fire often appears *dark* for a person inside the burning house. Thick, black smoke can hide the light of the flames, or the flames may be in another part of the house.

And fire is *quick!* In less than half a minute, a small flame can turn into a large fire. Within five minutes, a home may be totally ablaze. Fire safety experts say that only one to two minutes may be available for people to escape a house fire.

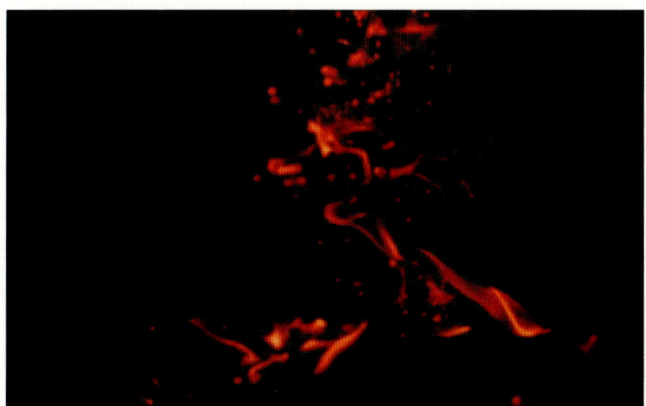

You may have less than two minutes to escape a burning house!

Contrary to what we may first think, the inside of a burning house is often dark because of heavy smoke. Could you find your way out of a house looking like this?

House fires are also *deadly.* Smoke and gases kill more people than the actual flames, by a ratio of three to one. This means that a fire at the other end of the house may asphyxiate a sleeping person.

Of course, house fires are also *hot.* Do you know how hot? At floor level the air may be only 100°F, but at head level for adults it may be a scorching 600°. Air this hot can literally scorch the lungs and instantly melt clothes to the wearer's skin.

Every day, on average, the American Red Cross responds to 180 home fires in the United States. Note that this is *not* the fire department, but the Red Cross, which provides clothes, food, furniture, and other essentials to victims of home fires. Many victims of home fires, however, will not contact the Red Cross, so the actual number of fires is much higher. The Red Cross reports that in the last two decades home fires have risen 10 percent in the United States.

Planning to have a house fire

The best way to deal with a house fire is to prevent it from happening. But sad to say, some people actually seem to be planning to have a house fire. That's right, by failing to plan to avoid a fire, you are actually planning to have one!

In the story "Scorched Kitchen for Breakfast," when the boys were sent for the fire extinguisher, they could not get it off the wall. How long would it have taken the father to teach his boys the correct way to get the fire extinguisher off the wall? Maybe one minute. In that case, his failure to give a one-minute lesson cost precious time—and could have cost their home.

At a very young age, children should be taught about fire escape plans. These plans can be simple, and children will enjoy helping to draw them.

Fire experts do not recommend that children use fire extinguishers. This is because children might lack the maturity to decide whether the extinguisher is capable of putting out the fire or not. They may also not be physically capable of handling the equipment. Young children should be taught to get out and stay out of a burning structure.

Review the following points about making a fire escape plan.

Depending on the ages and personalities of your children, you may need to adapt them to suit your needs.

- Draw a basic plan of the house, with at least two escape options given for each room.

- In upper stories, if the second option is a window with no roof to step out on, a collapsible escape ladder should be present. Teach your children how to use it.

- Make sure none of the windows included in the escape plan are stuck, and that any screens or security bars are easily removable.

- Have a designated place outside the home—preferably in the front—where all occupants will meet if a fire occurs. This helps eliminate the question of whether everyone is out of the house or not.

- Teach everyone that fires are often dark, so they may need to feel their way out of the house. Practice an escape from sleeping quarters with eyes closed or with the lights turned out at night.

- If any smoke is present, always get down close to the floor when escaping. Make this a part of practice escapes.

- Do not open any door that is hot to the touch.

- Fire experts recommend reviewing the fire escape plan twice a year.

- You may need to teach your children not to fear firefighters, who may enter their rooms to rescue them. With all their paraphernalia, firefighters may look like scary monsters coming to get them. Show the children pictures of firefighters, explaining who they are and that they are our friends.

- If possible, use sleeping quarters on the ground floor for those who have limited mobility and would need assistance in escaping. This would include older people, young children, and those with impaired mobility.

Show pictures like this to young children and tell them that firefighters are their friends, not some scary monsters!

Stop, drop, and roll

What should you do if, God forbid, your clothes catch fire before you are able to get out? There is one thing you *never* want to do: run. Running only feeds more oxygen to the fire, the same as if you were blowing on it. If you ever find your clothes on fire and you cannot easily slap it out, always remember the following words: STOP, DROP, and ROLL. If you can, put something over your hand while swatting so you do not burn your hand. Wrapping your whole body in a blanket, towel, or some other piece of cloth is another option.

But never, ever, run. If you must run a short distance to escape a burning structure, be sure to STOP, DROP, and ROLL as soon as you are out of danger.

Fire Extinguishers?—Give Me Four of Them!

In the United States, every 23 seconds a fire truck speeds away, sirens blazing and lights flashing, to a fire somewhere.[5] Some of these are house fires; others are vehicle fires, forest or grass fires, or fires in other structures besides houses. In 2018, an average of 10 Americans died each day because of a fire.[6] Others survived the fire but had painful burns and horrible memories.

Occasionally a fire begins with an explosion, but most begin as small, manageable fires that could easily be controlled with a fire extinguisher. But what if you don't have one?

That is what happened to Henry. He was

working out in the field with his skid steer when a small fire started in the engine compartment. Because the fire was located within the machine, he could not throw any dirt on it to smother it. To his disgust, he simply had to watch the fire consume the machine.

After the incident, he went to a local fire and safety business. "How much does a small fire extinguisher cost, one to carry on machinery?"

"About $50," replied the salesman.

"Give me four of them! I just lost a piece of machinery because I didn't have a fire extinguisher on board!" Henry exclaimed.

Perhaps you know there are several types of fire extinguishers, and it sounds confusing. Actually, it really is not that bewildering. Let's take a few minutes to learn about five different types of fires, and it will begin to make sense.

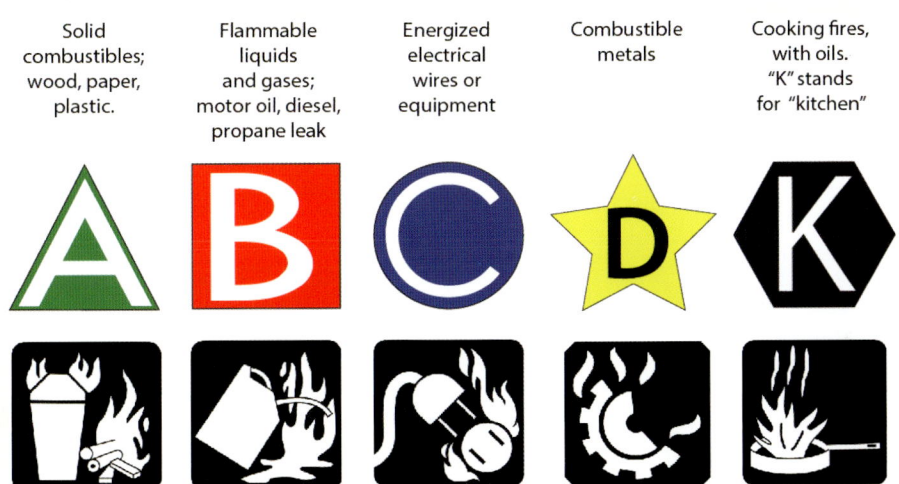

Remember the first four letters of the alphabet, and then the letter K. That's not too hard, is it?

Fire is fire, right? So there is really only one type of fire. But there are five classifications of *things that burn*. Depending on what is burning, different types of suppressants work better than others. For example, if you have an electrical fire, you do not want to use water, since the person squirting the water could receive an electrical shock if the electricity is still turned on.

Each type of fire has its own special needs. Class A, for example, may be hard to extinguish completely because of heat being held in the materials. The flames may be snuffed out, but the heat may cause the fire to reignite.

A Sound-Based Fire Extinguisher

Boom-thumpa, boom-thumpa, boom-thumpa, boom-thumpa . . .

You have probably heard—and felt!—the sounds belching from the oversized speakers in a vehicle going down the road. But did you know that those *boom-thumpas* are capable of putting out a fire?

While still in the research and development stage, two university students have proven that the thumping bass sounds of 30-50 Hz, if focused on a grease fire in a frying pan, could extinguish the flames. The two students found that higher frequencies had no effect on the flames, but the low frequencies were sufficient to snuff them out.

This technique could be developed into a fire extinguisher that would be mounted into the hood of a kitchen range. With sensors that determine when flames are present on the stovetop, the speakers would *boom-thumpa* the fire, extinguishing the flames!

Used on a larger scale, perhaps even forest fires could be fought with deep bass music. However, that is theoretical and may never be feasible. At this point, the technology has only been proven on fires less than 12 inches in diameter.

Spreading water on a Class B fire may only serve to spread the fire further. The burning liquids may float on the water, acting like a burning boat.

For Class C fires, the reason for not using water is obvious. Imagine a firefighter hosing down a live electrical box!

You will likely never see a Class D fire, but keep in mind that all metals do burn if they get hot enough. Aluminum, for example, will burn at 1,218°F. Imagine throwing water into such a hot fire. The result would be some kind of explosion.

Also avoid using water on a kitchen grease fire. When water is dumped onto a cooking oil fire, the water turns to steam instantly, blowing oil—and fire—in all directions.

Most home fire extinguishers are rated ABC. Check the extinguisher that is by the door of your house. If you do not have a fire extinguisher, get one immediately!

Check to see what type of fire the extinguisher is rated for.

Check to see if the pressure gauge is up.

Check to see how old the extinguisher is. Some models need to be test discharged and refilled periodically.

How about grabbing a fire extinguisher and finding it empty just when you need it? That would probably be worse than not having one at all.

Don't be like Henry, who decided that having four extinguishers would be better than having none—after it was too late!

PASS the extinguisher!

Now that we have learned about the different types of fire extinguishers, don't you think it would be good to learn how to use one so we aren't left scratching our heads when the fire is starting to burn down the house?

A fire extinguisher is really simple to use, but many people have never taken the time to learn how they operate. The secret is to **PASS** the extinguisher.

- **P** – **P**ull the pin that keeps the trigger from being accidentally actuated.
- **A** – **A**im at the base of the flames. The flames are not the source of the fire; they are the results of the fire.
- **S** – **S**queeze the trigger.
- **S** – **S**weep the extinguisher from side to side. This will allow the agent to spread, rather than just pile up in the middle of the fire and leave the edges burning.

Pull the pin

Aim at the base of the fire

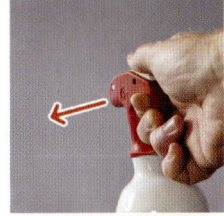

Squeeze the trigger

Sweep from side to side

Yes, it is that simple: Pull, Aim, Squeeze, Sweep . . . PASS the extinguisher.

Please Set My House on Fire!

Can you imagine people requesting that their house be set on fire? Our first thought might be of people who want to cheat their insurance company. But what about people who really do not want a fire, but ask for one anyway? It happens all the time. How? There might be a number of ways to do this, but one way is by using extension cords that are too small for the task they are made for.

This is what we do not want!

Just as a small water pipe can only carry a small amount of water, so a small electrical wire can only carry a small amount of electricity. For example, what happens when you try to push ten gallons of water through a drinking straw in ten seconds? Obviously, it will not happen. The straw would burst if we applied enough pressure to do that.

So it is with an electrical wire that is too small. As electricity passes through a wire, it creates friction, which builds up heat. A cheap household extension cord may have only thin 18-gauge wire. These wires are rated to carry seven amps (amperes) of current up to 25 feet.

How much is seven amps in layman's terms? It takes about 15 amps to run a typical room heater that you buy at the local department store, so this cord is not nearly heavy enough to run it. Many extension cords are made of 16-gauge wire, which can handle up to 10 amps. Still too small, right? What about a heavy-duty cord with 14-gauge wire that can handle up to 15 amps?

There is still a problem. Although the 14-gauge cord appears to be heavy enough to run the heater pulling 15 amps, it is still too small if the heater is running for hours on end. This is why the safety rule for using extension cords for room heaters is very simple: *NEVER do it. NEVER!* Air conditioners and refrigerators also pull heavy electrical loads, so the same rule applies: NEVER use an extension cord with these appliances.

While all extension cords are required by law to state the size of the conduit within them, most people pay little to no attention to that extremely important detail. An extension cord is an extension cord, right?

Not so! Failing to pay attention to the wire size is like ordering a house fire, just as you would order a pizza: one large fire, please, with charcoaled furniture, a coating of heavy black smoke, and an extra thick layer of ashes! And yes, it happens daily in the United States. In fact, electrical cords cause around 4,600 home fires a year, with 230 personal injuries and 70 deaths.[7] All because of an inadequate extension cord.

Consider the Martin family, who lived in a house trailer. They used an electric room heater to heat the far end of the trailer. After leaving home for the day, they were informed that their house was on fire. They rushed home to find that although the fire had been extinguished by the fire department before the house was entirely consumed, almost everything was ruined—either by fire, smoke, or water. The fire chief showed the family the frayed wires of an extension cord that had been used to run the room heater and explained that this had caused the fire. The cord had been placed under a rug to conceal it and to keep people from tripping over it.

You probably already know the safety rules that were violated in this true story. If not, continue reading to learn those rules and others. For the Martins, they learned the lesson the hard way.

Find the amps

By U.S. law, every electrical appliance and gadget must display how many amps it uses, either on a sticker or else molded or stamped onto the piece. For a practice session, let's look at a typical household extension cord and compare it to the amperage rating of some things people may use the cord to power.

First let's notice the cord, with a close-up of the wire size. As with all wires, the size of the conductor should be stamped onto its coating.

16 - 2

This wire says "#16 – 2." This means that the conductor is 16-gauge and runs through two wires. The following chart tells us how much electrical power can safely be used with this and other size cords, in both amps and watts. For those who enjoy math, the formula for calculating electrical volume is *Volts x Amps = Watts,* which can also be written as *Watts ÷ Volts = Amps.* A typical household electrical outlet is figured at 120 or 125 volts.

#18	7 Amps	840 Watts
#16	10 Amps	1,200 Watts
#14	15 Amps	1,800 Watts
#12	18 Amps	2,160 Watts

Now let's look at the information found on several items found in my own house and see whether our #16 cord is adequate.

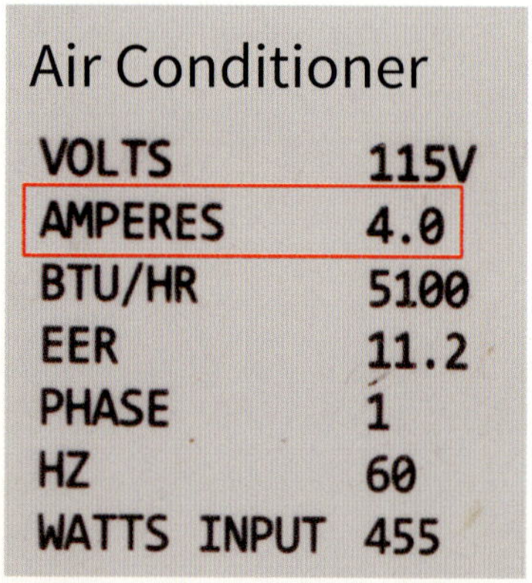

Air Conditioner
VOLTS 115V
AMPERES 4.0
BTU/HR 5100
EER 11.2
PHASE 1
HZ 60
WATTS INPUT 455

Laser Printer
110V-120V ~ 50/60Hz 9.0A

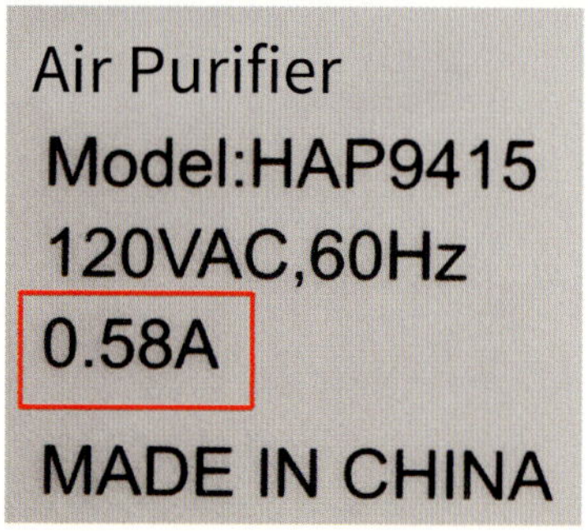

Air Purifier
Model: HAP9415
120VAC, 60Hz
0.58A
MADE IN CHINA

First let's consider a small air conditioner. Since this is one of the smallest air conditioners sold, it only pulls 4 amps. In this case, it should be safe to use this extension cord, although it is recommended never to use extension cords with air conditioners because they can run continuously for hours on end, with heat building up in the cord because of this extended use.

How about a laser printer? We find that our cord works but is close to the limit. It may be all right if used only for short times. The reason laser printers use so much electricity is because the toner is heated to make it melt into the paper. Any time electricity is used to create heat, the power usage jumps tremendously.

Now we come to an air purifier/filter. Since this appliance is not heating or cooling anything and only has a fan blowing air through a filter, the amperage use drops way down to less than one amp. We can use the cord with this appliance without any fear of overheating the cord.

And finally we come to a room heater. These heaters

are the culprit in many extension cord fires because they use a lot of power. In no way whatsoever would we want to use our extension cord with this appliance, which uses 1500 watts of power. Remembering our formula of watts ÷ volts = amps, we divide 1500 by 120 and find that this heater uses 12.5 amps—definitely too much for our #16 cord.

Heater
MODEL: CZ798
120VAC 60Hz
1500W

Additional safety tips for extension cords

- Never cover an extension cord with a rug. While this may keep people from tripping over the cord, the rug can hold in heat and cause a meltdown in the cord.

- Never run an extension cord across a walkway. People frequently trip over these.

- If a cord appears damaged or melted, do not use it.

- Extension cords are designed for temporary use. If you need a permanent electrical supply, add a properly wired outlet. According to the National Electric Code, no extension cord is rated for being run inside a wall.

- Watch for pinch points when routing a cord, such as under a piece of furniture, around a sharp corner, or through a hole in a cabinet.

- Do not remove the third prong (the ground prong) on a cord to make it fit into another cord or an old outlet. Use the proper cord or adapter. A two-prong extension cord is designed only for devices that do not require a ground prong.

Sprayed by Hot Foam

What boy doesn't like a good *boom* now and then? Aerosol cans thrown into the burn barrel provide just such *booms*. Have you ever wondered, though, what could happen if someone stood right beside the barrel when the explosion occurred?

Ruby knows. She knows first-hand. On a beautiful September day, she put a match to some trash from a remodeling project she was doing with her husband. Laths, wallpaper, paneling, and other burnable things had been put into one container on the porch, while non-burnables went into another.

Burned-out "missile."

Somehow an empty foam spray can ended up in the container of burnables. Ruby took the trash to the burn barrel and lit the match. Staying with the fire until it was blazing, she then turned to collect her empty container and return it to the porch. Just as she turned to leave, the foam can exploded—*BOOM!*

Hot foam flew in all directions and splattered onto her jacket, scarf, hair, and eyeglasses. It was so hot that some of her hair was singed, and her glasses were damaged. Thankfully, very little of the exploding foam hit bare skin.

Ruby was fortunate that her only losses were a pair of ruined glasses and a damaged scarf and jacket. But what if she had been looking toward the fire when the foam can exploded? She and her family are grateful to God for protecting her from such a tragedy.

The lesson is simple: *Keep all pressurized cans out of the burnable trash!* In this case, no one knows for sure how the can ended up in the burnable trash, but one of Ruby's small children may have mistakenly put it into the wrong container.

The Candle That Lit the Island

The tantalizing smell of the large candle burning on the kitchen island wafted through Andy's house. As a safety precaution, the family always placed the candle in a little platter that would catch the wax as it melted. Tonight Andy's family was gathered around the kitchen island as he told them a story.

Suddenly, right in front of their eyes, one side of the candle collapsed! An avalanche of hot, burning wax slid down the side of the candle. The melted wax continued to burn as it spilled over the edge of the platter. In mere seconds, a large portion of the island was covered with burning wax. Quickly the family ran for moist towels and extinguished the flames before any damage was done.

Andy described it as a phenomenon that most people will never see. He still shudders to think what could have happened if no one had been at home.

Never leave a lit candle unattended! According to the National Fire Protection Association, residential fires caused by candles are reported an average of 21 times a day in the United States, about one every hour. About 80 people die every year and another 677 are injured, with property losses equaling around $278 million. All because of candles![8]

An ex-fireman from an Ohio fire department reports that their small department always expected a home fire during the Christmas holidays, usually due to a candle. Many home candle fires also occur over New Year's Day. Here are some common-sense candle safety rules to keep in mind:

- Burn candles in a safe container so that if the wax does collapse, it remains enclosed.
- Check burning candles every few minutes.
- Never leave a room or go to bed with a candle burning unattended.
- The National Fire Protection Association recommends keeping burning candles at least 12 inches from anything flammable. Three out of every five home candle fires occur when the flame is placed too close to something. Be extra cautious when placing candles in windows, as blinds and curtains can swing into the flame due to air movement.
- Place the burning candle on a solid, hard surface rather than a soft one such as a towel or tablecloth.
- Always remember that candles are an open flame. Never burn a candle where fumes from kerosene, gas, or mineral spirits can reach it.
- Be careful about burning too many candles in a small space. In order for a fire to burn, it needs oxygen; too many candles in a small space can burn up the oxygen that people need to breathe.

- "Never play with fire!" That old saying certainly relates to candles. For this reason, never leave a small child alone in a room with a burning candle. The temptation for children to play with that flickering flame is very, very strong.

Candles are nice and they smell wonderful. But make sure you are familiar with the danger before you light one. As the saying goes, "Haste makes waste."

This photo represents a cozy scene, inviting us to read and relax. Let's take a look at any safety issues we see, as well as what is being done correctly.

- The candle is too close to a flammable pillow and fuzzy seating material. Also, are the curtains and blinds secured so that a breeze will not blow them into the flame?
- The candle is not on a stable surface. Could a slamming door topple it over?
- The matches have been left too close to the candle.
- Correct: The candle is in a glass container with tall sides so that no melted wax can create a fire hazard.

Chimney Fires

October came with its bright blue skies and colorful trees—such beauty as only God could create.

Along with the dazzling array of autumn colors came chilly nights. Mark went to the basement to fire up the wood stove for the first time that season. He and his family had moved into the house only the previous spring and had used the basement stove only a few times before warmer weather set in.

During the summer, he had accumulated a pile of old cardboard and paper to serve as fire starters. Now he filled the stove with some of this, put a few pieces of wood on top, and lit a fire. After opening the damper, Mark went upstairs.

A few minutes later when he went outdoors for something, he noticed the chimney was pouring out smoke like a steam engine. *Hmmm. There must have been some plastic in that cardboard that I didn't notice.* Paying no more attention, he went about his business.

About 15-20 minutes later, Mark was once again outside. The chimney was still spewing out smoke. *Something is wrong,* he thought, shaking his head. *If it was just some plastic in the cardboard, it would have burned up by now.*

Smoking like a steam engine.

Heading to the basement, he opened the stove door. A distinct *whooooooo* was coming from the chimney. Realizing that the roar was evidence of a chimney fire, he quickly shut the door, closed the damper, and shut off the air intake. The roar died down but did not stop completely.

The owner of the rented house had some chimney fire suppressors stashed nearby, so Mark opened the door of the stove and tossed them in. After shutting down the stove once more to prohibit oxygen intake, Mark went outside to see how much smoke was coming out. While the smoke output was reduced by at least 75 percent, it was still more than what it should have been. The brick chimney was cool to the touch, but now Mark noticed something alarming. Smoke was pushing out of small cracks in the mortar.

The fire seemed mostly under control, but the cracked mortar concerned him. What if there were other cracks on the side of the chimney that adjoined the wooden frame house? Pondering the situation, he decided it was better to be safe than sorry. He called 911 and reported the fire.

Within ten minutes, firefighters were on the scene. One firefighter made his way up the steep roof and dropped in a fire suppressant. He then used a weight tied to a chain to knock out the burning creosote. Men at the bottom of the chimney shoveled out the creosote from the cleanout at the bottom. After about an hour's work, the men were done.

"There was a huge amount of creosote in there," the fire chief reported to Mark. "We took out about a wheelbarrow load." His next news was worse: "That chimney is bad. We could see the flashes of the fire truck's red lights coming through the cracks when we peered down after putting out the fire. You shouldn't use that chimney anymore."

The chimney was about forty years old. Though no one would have noticed it from the outside, the chimney had long ceased being safe. Even in otherwise perfect circumstances when the heat could flow easily up the chimney, the small cracks could have let heat come into contact with the wood of the house.

The chimney fire didn't cause any damage to the house, and the fire department didn't charge for their services. Fortunately, the house had another wood stove upstairs with a new stainless steel chimney that was available to heat the house. The lesson for Mark that day was to always check for clogged chimneys before using a woodstove or fireplace.

- The first thing to do when you have a chimney fire is to shut down all the air intakes, including stove doors, ash cleanouts, and glass fireplace covers. Close the damper if there is one. This cuts down the available air to the fire in the chimney. In some cases, this may be enough to snuff out the fire, but more likely the fire will continue to smolder in the chimney. Leave the air intakes closed until the fire is completely out and the chimney has had time to cool off. Otherwise, the fire will likely begin blazing again.

- Chimney fire suppressants may help contain a chimney fire. The hot-burning suppressants burn up all the oxygen, thus suffocating the fire. In the case of an emergency, burnable road flares may help, as they burn hot like official chimney fire suppressants. In any case, if your chimney is on fire, do not hesitate to call 911 first and report it. It is better to have the fire department come to a fire that is already out than to come when it is too late.

- After the fire was under control, the fire chief told Mark that October sees more chimney fires than any other month. Since the weather has not turned very cold yet, people tend to use slow, smoldering fires to knock off the chill. The same thing happens in the spring as the days become warmer. Slow, smoky fires plug a chimney with creosote, creating the fuel for a chimney fire.

- Burning green (undried) firewood can also lead to chimney fires. If green wood is the only option, make sure the fire burns hot all the time. If possible, mix one piece of green wood with several pieces of dried wood. The best way is to simply never burn green wood.

- One simple method to help reduce creosote buildup is to burn a very hot fire with an open damper and air intake for 15-20 minutes every day. This lets lots of heat go up the chimney, drying up the creosote before it can accumulate.

- Check chimneys before each heating season and regularly during the season, especially if you are not burning hot fires.

- To check a chimney, use a mirror to look up into it. The sides of the chimney should not have any creosote buildup. If in doubt, also check from the top. Any creosote buildup thicker than one-fourth inch makes a chimney susceptible to a chimney fire.

Don't let this type of photo adorn your family photo album!
Check your chimneys regularly for creosote buildup.

Farm and Logging Safety

Blinded by His Own Knife

Seventeen-year-old Jonas worked quickly. The cows on his father's ranch at the foot of the Rocky Mountains needed to be fed. Bags of grain waited for someone to dump their contents into the feed troughs for the hungry cows. But first he had to cut the strings with which they were tied.

Putting the sharp knife under one string, he yanked up. *Slice!* Then the next one. *Slice!*

Then it happened. A string that was a bit tougher than the others needed an extra hard yank. Jonas put his teenage muscles to full work, and the knife finally ripped through the tough strings. But before he could stop it, the force of his upward yank sent the sharp knifepoint straight into his left eye!

The damaged eye did not have to be removed, but Jonas did lose his sight in it. He forever regrets his ignorance in the proper use of a knife. Yes, he was a "farm boy" who had used his pocketknife many times. But he learned too late the importance of pointing a knife away from yourself while cutting. *Never use your biceps to cut!* He often tells those he meets about the accident, hoping to prevent another young boy from having a blind eye for the rest of his life.

Where Are the Children?

In Christian homes, Mom generally tends the small children in the home while Dad labors to supply the family's needs. On occasion, though, Mom needs to be gone and Dad gets the privilege of tending his children. In farm situations, this often means the children get to tag along with Dad while he does all kinds of exciting things.

In the days before mechanized equipment, children watched their father mow hay with a scythe, pick corn by hand, or split rails to make a fence. But on today's farms, they often watch Dad as he cleans the barn with a skid steer, moves large bales of hay with a front-end loader, or spreads manure with a 150-horsepower tractor.

The transition to large equipment has happened over several generations, and we often forget how easy it is to run over children with farm equipment. Years ago the danger was much smaller. Think about it—a farmer has gone from hauling manure with a pitchfork and an open wagon, or even a wheelbarrow, to jumping into a large tractor pulling a 9,500-gallon liquid manure tank.

Climbing into the driver's seat, today's farmer will often have to ask himself, "Where are the children? Are they playing hide-and-seek?" If he were using a wheelbarrow to move his manure, or even a team of horses, the chances of a child getting run over would be much smaller.

An important foundation

Fathers training their children by working alongside them is something we never, ever want to lose. Of course, for safety reasons the father needs to wait until the child is old enough to understand the dangers of whatever task is at hand. A small child can easily help haul manure to the garden with a wheelbarrow, but if the manure is being moved by large equipment, he will need to wait.

An important consideration is why the child is with the father. Is he training the child? Or is he just babysitting while Mom shops?

A father who is training a child is more likely to think of safety because he considers the child part of the project. But if the child is an "add-on" to his work schedule, he is more likely to get caught up in his task and forget that he has children to keep track of . . . somewhere.

One Mennonite man who promoted home safety among his church group made the following observation: On today's farms with large equipment, children should not be allowed to accompany Dad to work unless he is *training* his children, not just *babysitting*.

Keeping that distinction in mind will not guarantee that an accident will not happen. But the chances are greatly reduced if the babysitting Dad suspends his work with large equipment until someone else can take over watching the little ones. Remember, our farming lifestyle has changed in the last few generations, and we want to keep our children safe while we pass on our work ethic to them.

These three graphics show the progress of liquid manure spreading. When we think of children helping Dad spread manure—and actually participating in the work—which scene is most likely to represent that opportunity? Consider the speed of the equipment and the ability of a child to get out of harm's way while playing near the equipment.

To be sure, the bottom photo would be safest—if the child is securely settled in an approved rider seat of the tractor. But think of the amount of exercise he will get if he just rides along without doing anything except watching the equipment at work.

83

Bulls, Rams, and Bucks

One of my first memories of the dangers of male animals on the farm occurred when I was about six years old. My younger brother, who was three years old, was walking with my dad and me and other family members toward a pile of old manure just outside the barn. Two or three feet high and about eight feet in diameter, the mound caused a great temptation for my three-year-old brother. Picking up speed, he ran toward the pile and began his ascent.

The ram came from behind just as my little brother neared the peak. We watched in surprise as the ram made contact just as my brother reached the top, giving him an extra ride he did not expect! I am sure the ram did not plan his actions, but he did a good job of timing it just right to send my brother airborne.

Of course, my little brother, who was crying, did not think it was funny. Actually, none of us did at the time. Dad soon comforted my brother, who thankfully was not hurt. He then disciplined the erring ram.

My next bad memory of male animals on the farm happened when I was around twenty years old. An elderly acquaintance went into his son-in-law's pasture to cut firewood. I don't know if he knew a bull was in the field or not, but later in the day they found him dead in the pasture, with his chainsaw lying nearby.

Then there was the *gaucho*[1] in South America who acted foolishly. On an isolated ranch in Bolivia, I helped this cowboy as they vaccinated their cattle. Running the cattle through the chutes made of poles cut from the woods, we finally got to the bull. The gaucho was probably in his 40s, and you could tell he knew how to handle cattle. When the bull's turn came, the gaucho stayed right there *inside* the chute, with only a sharpened stick as a tool. The bull would lower his head menacingly, but the gaucho just kept poking him in the nose with the stick to hold him back. He would then look over at me and grin; he was having fun!

Thankfully, the gaucho survived his foolhardiness, and the bull got his shot just like the cows. But it was certainly an unwise thing to do.

Now for the final sad bull story that comes to my mind. A distant cousin of mine lies six feet under the dirt. Barely into his twenties, he had taken up bull-riding. It did not end well for him. He took one too many chances, all for the glory of a few seconds of

---

[1] A South American cowboy.

excitement and the applause of the crowd.

Despite the danger, I have seen huge bulls led around like a puppy on a string. If these "gentle" beasts are raised from small calves, they will often recognize and trust their caretakers.

But male farm animals can never be fully trusted. They are "programmed" to run on instinct. That instinct can be trained, but at any time the instinct to protect may override the fear and respect that men try to put into them.

Let's look at this from a slightly different angle. A few weeks ago my wife noticed something strange in the field, something flopping around about a hundred yards from our house. With binoculars, we could see it was a large bird of some kind, and we could also see our cat sitting close by—just a few feet away—trying to make sense of all this flopping about.

Grabbing a camera, I hurried out to see what was going on. Imagine my surprise as I approached to find out that this was not a wounded bird, but two red-tailed hawks fighting with each other. Claws grasped, they would peck at each other and flop around. Then they would tire and relax for a moment before resuming their fight.

The interesting thing about this, and the part that ties into this article on the danger

These two hawks lost their fear of humans during the fight. The same loss of fear can happen at any time with a male farm animal.

of male farm animals, is that they were so intent on fighting each other that they let me approach to within about six feet of them. Under normal circumstances, there is no way you could approach that close to a red-tailed hawk.

The point is that *their protection instinct overran their normal fear of man.* They were, I assume, in a territorial dispute. It likely began in the air, but then they came down to finish the dispute on the ground.

This applies to farm animals. What is usually a gentle, sweet bull, ram, or buck may quickly turn into an angry male intent on protecting its territory, even to death. I don't know if the hawks would have fought to death; I purposely broke them up shortly after arriving. But I'm sure they *wanted* to kill each other!

Now take that same anger and place it into a farm animal. This time the anger is not against another animal, but against a person who is threatening his territory. The rule is simple: *Never trust a male farm animal.*

Most victims of bull accidents have had prior experience with bulls and just simply forgot how dangerous they can be. Often the most aggressive bulls are those raised on-site.

Would you like the grazing bull pictured below to consider you an invader in his territory? I certainly wouldn't want to meet those horns swinging around in fury!

Never trust a bull. Not even if you raised it from a calf. At any time their instinct to protect their territory may suddenly override their previous respect for you.

Almost Gassed to Death

After a busy Friday and Saturday, half of the silo was filled with ryelage (rye fodder). On Sunday morning, David and his wife Ellen attached the milking machines while their ten-year-old son Nevin went up into the silo to see why the unloader was stuck. Since the ryelage had settled overnight, they also needed to know how far to let it down. Stepping into the silo room, David started lowering the unloader a couple of cranks at a time. Communicating by two-way radio, Nevin would tell his father when to let it down a few more cranks.

After a little bit, Nevin radioed his father. "Start the blower. It stinks up here." This should have been a warning sign, but David was unaware that ryelage gas was dangerous.

A short time later, David suddenly heard a strange sound come over the two-way radio, something like a distressed moan. *Oh, no, Nevin must be stuck in the auger!* David thought. Only later did they realize that Nevin had tried to inform his father to shut off the unloader.

Yelling to Ellen, who was still in the milking parlor, David quickly informed her of the situation. "Nevin is caught in the unloader! I'm going up!"

Rushing up the silo chute, David found that Nevin was *not* caught in the unloader, nor was he unconscious. David realized that Nevin was not physically injured, and then the reality of silo gas hit him.

Yelling down to Ellen, David instructed, "Start the tractor and blower, then go up the outside of the silo and close the lid!" Closing the lid would force more fresh air from the blower down into the silo.

With that, David entered the silo to try to get Nevin into the chute. This did not go well at all. Nevin was still conscious, but not "with it" and fought his father's attempt to rescue him.

By the time David had wrestled Nevin over to the chute, he himself was close to being overcome with the gas. Squeezing himself and Nevin into the chute—they barely fit in together—David set them into a freefall, lightly catching a step occasionally to slow them. But because they fit so tightly, the 20- to 30-foot slide down the chute did not hurt them.

At the bottom, they landed in the feed cart. Other than a few faint moans, Nevin was barely responding anymore. With Ellen still up on the silo, David called 911 and reported a silo gas incident but specified that neither victim was entrapped anymore.

But somehow the incident got reported to the various emergency agencies as a full-blown entrapment. After a short time, all kinds of emergency personnel began to show up. Heading back to the silo room, David was feeling refreshed enough to get Nevin out of the feed cart. By this time, Nevin was starting to come around. By the time the ambulances arrived, he was walking around, although full mental capacity did not return all at once.

The first ambulance took Nevin, with Ellen riding along. Then it was David's turn, even though he wasn't feeling dizzy anymore. After a few hours in the hospital, both were released. Neighbors helped finish the morning milking and then also did the evening milking.

Lessons David learned . . . the hard way

- David says his biggest takeaway is the realization that rye and other small grain forage crops can also make silo gas. Although corn silage makes *more* silo gas than most other crops, any fermenting crop can make dangerous gases.

- Both David and Nevin were feeling fairly well by the time the ambulances arrived. Would they have had to go to the hospital? David firmly believes that it was good that they did so. He is now aware of others who were caught in silo gas and have experienced long-term lung issues. David feels they were spared long-term damage because they were given oxygen and immediate treatment.

- Some of the doctors at the hospital did not even know what a silo was, let alone silo gas. And this was in a farming community. In these situations, someone may need to educate the medical profession about what has occurred and what should be done for the victim.

Silo gas safety

- Any forage that ferments can and will produce silo gases. The first two or three days after filling a silo are the worst for producing nitrogen dioxide (a mixture of nitrates and oxygen). This gas can kill a person within just three minutes of exposure. Among all forage crops, corn and sorghum top the list, although some weeds are even worse. To cut back on excess nitrates that can add to more silage gases, do not over-fertilize crops with nitrogen. Also, the bottom parts of the plant have the heaviest concentrations of nitrates, so raising the cutter and leaving 12 inches of stubble in the field can reduce nitrate levels in silos.

- The recommendation is to stay out of silos for 21 days after filling. The first two or three days are the worst, and by 10 days the gases should no longer be forming. However, the gases can remain in the silo for several days after forming.

- If you must enter a newly filled silo, first run the blower for 15 to 20 minutes to blow out any gases. Be aware that if the silo is less than half full, the gases may not be moved out efficiently by the blower. Wear a self-contained breathing apparatus when entering a recently filled silo. And *never* enter a silo without having someone else nearby to be of aid if necessary.

- Nitrates of oxygen gases are heavier than air, so they will settle to just above the level of the silage. If the chute doors are open at that level, the gases may settle down into the silage room, and from there can drift into the barn. These gases can kill livestock as well as humans.

- Keep silo rooms ventilated well after filling the silo. A good rule of thumb is simply to stay out of the silage room until the danger of nitrogen dioxide gas has passed.

- Keep children and visitors away from potentially gassed areas, which may mean locking doors and posting signs to barricaded areas to remind everyone to stay out.

Dilemma in the Manure Pit

Manure pit deaths are some of the saddest in the agricultural industry. Why? Because 40 percent of all manure pit deaths occur when someone goes into a pit to rescue someone else. This means that instead of one death, there are two, or even more. And it means that someone loved someone else enough to risk his life to try to rescue the person.

But that leaves a question lingering in our minds. When is it the right thing to try to rescue someone, knowing that we are taking a great risk? Is it really worth taking the risk when it may leave a family grieving for two or more missing members when it could have been only one?

These are hard questions—questions that this book cannot address with simple answers. Yet we will probe a little deeper into this dilemma after reviewing some manure pit safety guidelines.

A number of manure pit-related deaths have occurred in our Anabaptist communities in the last few decades, and most farmers are aware that unseen and often odorless gases lurk in these pits—deadly ones. Some of these gases can even explode and cause fires when an unknowing or unthinking person decides to grind or weld something close to the pit.

That brings us to the first safety point. Even if we are aware of the dangers of manure pit gases, we must not assume that everyone who comes to the farm will be. Repairmen, neighbors, relatives, and friends who drop by and help with the chores also need to be aware of the danger. Pits should be fenced and marked with warning signs. Obviously, we may not need the sign for ourselves, but what about the children of our visitors, who may be running around having a great time exploring the farm? Young boys might delight in stirring the manure with sticks.

Do the visiting boys on your farm know the dangers of manure pits? Or will they climb the fence and try to retrieve their ball with a stick?

At some point, every pit will need to be entered for some reason or another, even if just for periodic inspection. But never enter a pit unless you absolutely must. And when you do enter, have someone watching from a safe place and with the appropriate rescue gear.

While it is possible for a grown man to pull another grown man around in a pit with a rope, safety organizations recommend that any rescuer entering the pit wear a harness with a rope or cable attached. This rope or cable should be connected to a mechanical lifting device such as a winch, hoist, or pulley. This is especially important if the pit walls are vertical, and lifting a grown man up and out may not be possible for someone using only his physical strength.

For enclosed pits, proper ventilation is an absolute must before anyone even thinks of entering. Use a gas tester before entering a manure pit. Even with ventilation, a self-contained breathing apparatus is recommended for enclosed manure storage areas.

Remember, you cannot see the gases, and some of them you cannot smell. Sometimes it takes only seconds before the gases overwhelm your ability to think clearly. You may be physically able to move around, but your brain will become foggy. In such a condition, you may not even remember what you need to do to get out. After this, you will soon also start to lose your physical ability to move.

Methane gases are flammable, and an explosion can literally lift the roof off your barn if they are ignited. This can be caused by sparks in the fan motor or by activities such as welding, cutting, or grinding metal around manure pits.

Back to the dilemma

In 1989, a tragic accident occurred in a manure pit owned by a farmer in Michigan. The pit measured about twenty feet on each side and was around ten feet deep. One day the farmer's 28-year-old son went into the pit to replace a sheared pin on an agitator shaft. While crawling back out of the pit, he was overcome by the gases and fell back in. It was a multi-generational farming operation, and the farmer's 15-year-old grandson witnessed the fall. Quickly he entered the pit to try to rescue his uncle, but he also collapsed.

After this, two other members of the extended family and then finally the farmer himself tried their hand at rescuing the others from the pit. The fumes were simply too strong and each would-be rescuer collapsed because of the gases. Now there were five unconscious people in the pit.

Somehow a carpet installer who was at their house found out about the situation. He also entered the pit to try to rescue the others. He too was overcome, but his helper was able to get him back out.

At some point, the owner of a local farm implement business arrived with two other men. Using ropes, they were able to pull out the five farm workers. However, by the time the emergency squad arrived, the farmer's nephew had died. The remaining four were taken to emergency rooms, but the farmer and his younger son died on the way. The 15-year-old grandson died six hours later, and in the end the other son also died.

Five dead men, all from one family. Was it worth their valiant efforts?

Only those who have been through such a situation can know the agony of making that most difficult decision. In reading these stories from the safety of our armchairs, many of us will say we would be willing to risk our life to save someone, at least to a certain point. But where is that point?

Some situations are obvious. A 14-year-old son who sees his 180-pound father lying in a manure pit with 8-foot vertical walls should know that he will never—barring a miracle—be able to lift his father out of such a pit. On the other hand, if the pit has sloping sides he may be able to do it.

This uncertainty can cause a dilemma! While we cannot give a final answer for every situation, the following questions are some points to ponder before the tragic situation confronts us.

- First, are we taking all reasonable measures to prevent these situations?

- Is our walk with God up-to-date and healthy so that when a desperate situation arises, we can call upon Him for wisdom and expect an answer? These are difficult decisions that require divine help.

- Is trying to rescue someone we love, and then dying for it, as heroic as refraining when it looks impossible? Is it perhaps more heroic in some cases to stay alive for others who would be left behind?

- Is God going to judge us harshly in these difficult emergency situations for having made a bad judgment call one way or another?

- Should we judge others who have been in these situations, either for not being brave enough or being too brave?

After all is said and done, no human can tell us where that point is when we should try or not try to rescue someone. We need to be aware of the risks and keep the above safety points in mind before attempting to rescue someone from a manure pit. We do not want to be ignorant of the dangers.

We can greatly reduce the chances of finding ourselves in such a dreadful dilemma by putting up fences and warning signs and obeying common-sense safety regulations concerning manure pits.

Grain Engulfment: It Only Takes Two Seconds

While the number of agricultural accidents has trended down in the last decades, can you guess which type of accident has gone up? You probably know by the title: grain engulfment.

In flowing grain, just two seconds is enough to trap a person up to the knees. They may not be submerged, but they usually cannot get out by their own strength. Furthermore, in some cases a person can become totally submerged in as little as ten seconds if the grain keeps flowing (because of someone failing to turn off an auger, for instance).

Would you enter a grain bin full of quicksand? Probably not. But did you know that flowing grain has been likened to quicksand? The pressure on the body from the surrounding grain can suffocate a person even if his head is still above the surface.

Why not just put a pulley on the top of the bin, tie a rope around the person, and use a tractor to lift him out? Do NOT try this. The pressure on the body is so great that in at least one case it dislocated the victim's shoulder. Just "lifting them out" is not possible, except in the most minor cases. To lift a person buried to the waist requires 600 pounds of lifting pressure, plus the weight of the person being lifted. For a totally buried person, the required force can be more than 2,000 pounds to lift him out.

Grain engulfments are more common than you may think. Since 1965, an average of 19 per year have been reported in the United States. However, those numbers are just the ones *reported*; researchers feel certain that the actual numbers are higher. Unfortunately, the numbers are *increasing*. In 2010, for example, 51 entrapment incidents were reported. This increase is likely due to the higher percentage of farms that are storing grain on their farms. About 70 percent of all entrapments reported are on small, family-sized farms.[9]

It is not just in grain bins that entrapments occur, as 140 of the entrapment deaths have been in wagons or other farm equipment. Sadly, 95 percent of these deaths were boys under the age of eleven.[10]

What does that last statistic scream out to us? *Keep your children out of the wagons and trucks as you are loading and unloading!* I know; it is fun for the children. I well remember the joy as a boy playing in the gravity wagon as it unloaded. Actually, it was our job to kick down the corn, which was mostly on the cob in those days. Also, the wagons were little compared to today's grain carts, so that made it safer. But do not start bad habits. Letting children play in a wagon or cart while loading and unloading grain is a very bad habit.

Prevention: the best cure

The best way to cut down on entrapments is to have a simple rule called "zero entry." This means that no one—meaning *no one*—should enter a grain bin containing grain unless it is absolutely necessary. When such a necessity does arise, always make sure the person entering the bin is harnessed and that a suitable cable and other components are securely anchored to the bin wall. Be careful not to anchor the cable to a ladder, as the pull on an entrapped person in flowing grain could be too much for the ladder. Make sure someone is always watching from an entry door when someone is in a bin. And of course, always turn off the auger before entering a bin.

Three common errors

The following graphic shows three mistakes people tend to make in grain bins.

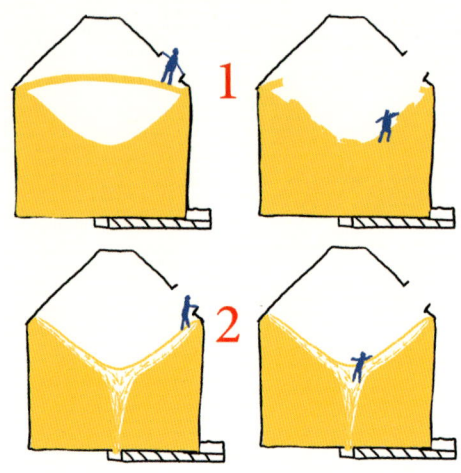

- In the first scenario, a worker enters a bin without realizing that a cap, also known as a crust or bridge, has formed and that the grain underneath has fallen away, leaving a pocket. The cap/bridge/crust finally breaks when the worker puts his weight on it, dropping him down into the grain. If the auger is on, the situation will be worse, because the second situation then comes into play. Once the grain fully engulfs a person, the survival rate is less than 10 percent.

- In the second scenario, the worker enters the bin with the auger running. He does not realize that the grain empties from the top down, and that the top few inches of grain flow fast. If he lets go and starts sliding down into the grain, he can quickly be sucked down into the center vortex.

- In the last scenario, a worker has entered a bin to pull down grain that is sticking to the sides of the bin. The grain on the side collapses, burying him in the process.

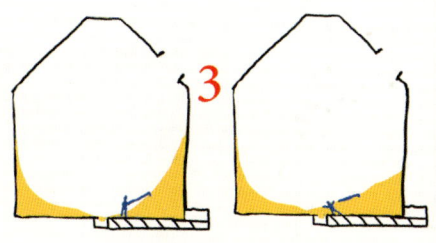

A fourth situation, less common, happens when suction equipment is used to empty a bin. If the operator of the suction hose is not careful, he can become trapped in a hole if he allows the hose to suction grain out near his feet.

Grain bin safety

To prevent caps or bridges from forming and grain from sticking to the bin sides, it is essential to store grain properly. The details of the storage process is beyond the scope of this book, but the basic safety guideline is to keep the grain well dried and ventilated during storage. Any moisture coming in can cause the grain to stick and clump together. If a crust does form, or if grain is sticking to the edge of a bin, try to deal with the issue from the outside, using a pole. Also remember that fermenting grains can release poisonous gases. Check gas and oxygen levels before entering the grain bin.

Place warning signs at grain bin entries. You may already understand the danger, but suppose relatives come for a family day and the boys climb into the bin to play hide-and-seek? Teaching workers and children the dangers of moving grain should be part of every farm safety program.

To the rescue

If someone does become entrapped in grain within a bin, *never* turn on the auger to try to empty the grain from around the victim. Doing so usually makes the situation worse, sometimes very quickly.

Immediately turn on ventilation fans, remembering not to cool the victim too much if the outside air is cold. Call for help, though in some farming communities professional help for bin rescues may not be readily available. Unless the person is barely submerged, trying to dig someone out of a grain entrapment often makes matters worse and wastes precious time.

Pushing a barrel with both ends cut out down around a grain entrapment victim may help keep him from becoming totally engulfed. Plywood and sheet metal have also been used successfully. Trained rescuers sometimes have specially built equipment to perform a release, but not all farm communities have trained rescuers available.

Try to place something around the victim to keep more grain from pressuring against him. If available, place a round tube around the victim, such as a 55-gallon drum with both ends cut out. You can also try sheets of plywood or metal. Take great caution to keep more grain from coming down while attempting to place the restraint over the person. Also, any rescuers should be harnessed while working so there won't be two entrapments instead of one. Stand on a piece of plywood to avoid making matters worse by your movements.

Panic in the victim only makes matters worse. If possible, keep someone near him to give reassurance while seeking help.

Once a barrel or other restraint material is in place, a partially submerged victim can be freed by carefully scooping out the grain inside the barrel. For deeply submerged people, rescuers will probably not be able to push the barrel down far enough. But at least some of the grain can be removed to allow the victim's body more room to function.

The next option is to cut V-shaped holes in the sides of the grain bin to allow the grain to flow away from the entrapped person. Cut the holes a couple of feet below the entrapped person. (If you cut too low, it can make the person sink in deeper as the grain drains away.) Make sure the holes are cut equally around the bin so the bin does not become off-balanced if too much grain drains out of one side. If no tool is available to cut notches in the bin, as a last resort try ramming the bucket of a skid steer into the side.

No farmer likes to see his bin ruined and the grain flowing out onto the ground, but that may be the only option if a life is at stake. Even a partial engulfment can quickly cause low blood pressure in the bottom parts of the victim's body, which may lead to amputation or, in the worst cases, death.

Remember, grain entrapments may be more common than you think. An average of around three per month occurred in the United States in 2019, and those are just the reported cases.[11] Don't make that average go up: *practice zero entry!*

Burned by the Drinking Cup

One December evening while her older siblings milked the 45 cows, Sarah decided to get a drink at the handwashing sink in the barn. At two and a half years old, she had to reach up over her head to grab the 12-ounce Rubbermaid drinking cup sitting on the sink. What little Sarah did not know was that the cup did not contain water, but a pre-measured amount of alkaline pipeline cleaner!

She put the cup to her lips and took a drink. Her immediate reaction was to splutter and spit. *Ugh! Yuck!*

Instantly the body's natural reaction to the ingestion of strong chemicals kicked in, and she began to produce large amounts of saliva.

Her siblings took the crying and drooling little Sarah to the house, where her parents, Mark and Andrea, tried to rinse out her mouth by holding her over the sink in the running water. Questions rushed through their minds. They tried to get her to drink milk. What should they do? Sarah had stopped crying, but she was still drooling excessively.

Quickly they drove to the emergency room, where the doctor put Sarah on a ventilator and ordered her taken to a regional hospital. Mark and Andrea followed at legal speed, which meant that Sarah had already been admitted to the pediatric intensive care unit when they arrived.

An esophageal scope revealed second-degree chemical burns on the esophagus, along with a couple of mild stomach burns. Stomach acids had neutralized the alkaline cleaner at that point. Sarah's mouth also suffered some burns, including a small burn on her chin.

After six days, Sarah was released, with an appointment to check back to the hospital in one week. During the week at home, she was able to swallow liquids but could not eat very well. Despite everything, she was happy and contented, with little or no complaining about pain or hunger.

When the week was up, Mark and Andrea took their precious daughter back for the checkup. The doctor's advice was ominous: the esophagus was constricting, and he wanted surgery soon—tomorrow! They needed to insert a gastric feeding tube, and then they planned to dilate Sarah's esophagus every two to four weeks to stretch it.

Not too long after that, at a checkup, the doctor broke the news to Mark and Andrea that Sarah's esophagus was damaged beyond repair. She needed replacement surgery. The instructions seemed gloomy: try to fatten Sarah up and pick a date within several months for the five-hour surgery.

A late April date was chosen, so the family enjoyed about two months of "normal" life. Sarah's parents were still optimistic. "Watch for a miracle!" they told the surgeon. In the end, the miracles were that Sarah survived—that she only needed two incisions instead of three, that her voice nerves were not damaged, and that she did not need a trachea operation. Despite these positives, when Sarah came out of surgery with tubes and wires attached all over her body, things looked depressing from Mark and Andrea's point of view.

The following weeks held many ups and downs, including much fervent prayer. One month later, Sarah was finally given permission to eat solid foods. This was a relief after so much time of using the feeding tube. Sarah was delighted to be able to eat "real" food with the rest of the family.

However, as time progressed, Mark and Andrea noticed that Sarah was having an increasingly difficult time getting her food down. So they scheduled an appointment to conduct another swallow test. The test revealed that the new esophagus, made from stomach tissue, was constricting. It was shrinking as it healed.

In the months that followed, the doctors performed more than ten stretches on Sarah's new esophagus. After that, Mark and Andrea were given the equipment to do the stretches at home. These started out daily for the first month, but then gradually had to be done less often.

When Sarah was six years old, she announced to her mother that the dilations were no longer necessary. "Why?" asked Andrea.

"God healed me, and we are all done!" was the reply.

Mark and Andrea discussed the situation and decided to honor Sarah's faith. Sarah was later released from all doctors' care some six years after the incident. She still has occasional difficulty swallowing, and because she is missing a valve at the top of her stomach, she must sleep inclined. Otherwise she is a healthy and active young lady.

What do Mark and Andrea have to say today after that long, complicated story? "NEVER use a regular drinking cup to measure chemicals." Andrea says. "NEVER!"

Mark and Andrea give glory to God for Sarah's recovery, and they give thanks to their family in Christ for assisting them through their trial. Through the help of others, they were able to pay off a nearly $300,000 hospital bill—a bill that was all because of one little swallow from what looked like a normal drinking cup.

In 2019, poison control centers in the United States gave guidance for around 2.1 million poison exposures. That means approximately every fifteen seconds someone swallowed or came into contact with a dangerous chemical.[12]

Farm chemical safety

- Never use a cup that looks like a drinking vessel to measure or store chemicals.
- Always punch holes in empty chemical containers so no one can use them for other purposes.
- Place chemicals behind a solid barrier out of a child's reach. This is recommended over storing them on a high shelf where they can still be seen. If the child sees them, he might find a stool to access them.
- Antifreeze has a sweet taste, and a child could mistake if for some kind of juice. Treat antifreeze as a dangerous chemical, and NEVER leave an open container of antifreeze standing around. It is also dangerous to pets, especially dogs.
- When transporting dangerous chemicals, secure them to the vehicle. In an accident, you do not want poisonous liquids flying all over the place. Even in normal travel, a bump in the road could easily cause a spill.
- Do not transport dangerous chemicals in glass containers; there is too much danger of breaking.
- Use safety glasses and gloves when handling chemicals.

Did you know that a gallon of gasoline has the potential force of seven sticks of dynamite? This is why you should never keep gasoline in a fragile container, especially not when transporting it. Always keep a lid on the container so that a stray spark cannot light any fumes. Do not store gasoline in your workshop!

- Make a list of potentially harmful chemicals on your farm and in the house, then decide if you are being prudent in how you store and handle them. Are they safely stored away from curious children? This includes rat poison, chlorine, antifreeze, cleaners, glues, hydrogen peroxide, gasoline, propane tanks, herbicides and pesticides, medicines, fertilizers, lubricants, etc.

- Keep the phone number for poison control beside your home telephone and/or add it to your cell phone contact list. The number for the U.S. Poison Control Center is 1-800-222-1222.

Crushed Head . . . and Heart!

Warm, sunny days in June are a delight for farmers. The hay is growing and the corn is peeking out of the soil in neat rows in the fields. Cows graze contentedly in the lush pastures, while calves jubilantly kick their heels nearby. Yes, June is a great time to be a dairy farmer.

It was just such a day in June of 1990 that Doris wanted to plant some watermelons in the garden. She gave instructions for her 8-year-old daughter Joyce to watch 15-month-old Dorothy and told all the children to play nicely in the yard. Seeing that things were in order with the children, she disappeared into the garden to plant the seeds.

A few minutes later her husband Ben came driving in the lane with a tractor pulling a manure spreader full of sawdust that he had just purchased from a nearby sawmill, with plans to put it in the steer pen. Ben deftly backed the manure spreader into the pen and began to unload the contents. The children, always eager to watch Daddy at work, came to the gate and stood peering in, just a few feet from Dad.

With the unloading task finished, Ben pulled the tractor and manure spreader forward, his children standing just a few feet away. Lined against the side of the shed, they did not appear to be in any danger. Climbing off the tractor to shut the gate, Ben realized that little Dorothy was fussing. He shut the gate and went to gather his precious daughter in his arms.

A wet diaper! No wonder the little girl was whimpering. Returning Dorothy to her place beside Joyce, Ben decided to park the tractor in the shed before he changed the diaper. Jumping on the tractor, he put it in gear and began to pull ahead . . . all without looking back. Unknown to him, Dorothy had followed him, while the other children looked on.

Ben drove about twenty feet when he felt the manure spreader hit a bump. It jerked the tractor, and he heard an unusual squeak. Looking back, his heart made a mighty leap as it hit him full force. The wheel of the 2,000-pound manure spreader had run squarely over little Dorothy's head and right shoulder! A grisly cry of, "Oh, no!" escaped his throat. Time seemed to stand still as he yanked the tractor out of gear and hit the ground running to where his small daughter lay face down in the driveway. Dorothy whimpered as she struggled to rise from the gravel. Ben scooped her up into his arms.

Meanwhile, Doris heard Ben's distressed cry in the garden and came running to the scene. Realizing that Dorothy was indeed still living, Ben carried her into the house and changed her diaper while Doris called an ambulance. During the wait for the ambulance, Dorothy deteriorated right in front of Ben's eyes, causing him to become frantic.

In the hospital, Dorothy "coded"—meaning her heart stopped beating and she quit breathing. The doctors and nurses worked frantically. Very soon their efforts were rewarded by the little heart starting to beat again.

A series of tests and surgery followed, showing that the weight of the manure spreader had fractured Dorothy's nose and severed a nerve in the right side of her face, which resulted in paralysis on that side of her face. Additionally, she lost sight in her right eye, and her right ear had a cracked cochlea, which resulted in complete loss of hearing in that ear. After seven days in the hospital, little Dorothy was able to come back home.

The accident caused initial brain damage, and Dorothy had to learn to walk again, which took about a month. But her brain has healed, and today Dorothy is a functional, bright young lady. However, she has never recovered the sight in her right eye or the hearing in her right ear, nor lost the partial face paralysis. These conditions have indeed caused some barriers in her life, but she has learned to overcome them and live a full life.

While the consequences of the crushed head have been a hindrance in Dorothy's life, the physically unseen consequences of a crushed heart have plagued Ben for many years.

A small mistake has laid a large load of guilt upon his heart.

First, even though they did so in an orderly fashion, he allowed his children to stand too close to his work. Second, he failed to look back when starting off with the tractor and manure spreader. And third, he had not attended to the dirty diaper right away.

The years have helped to ease the burden of the many "what ifs" on his crushed heart. But the scene is forever etched into his mind . . . a scene he hopes no one else ever has to experience.

"Is it clear to back up? Where did the children get to? They must have gotten bored watching me and have gone away to play."

But maybe their favorite kitty is under the spreader, and they are quickly trying to rescue it before Dad backs over it.

Do not move the equipment until all the children are accounted for!

Rolled Alive

Ivan turned the wheat drill around at the end of the row as he finished seeding the field. It was the first part of May, and the Canadian planting season had come.

Riding on the back of the John Deere drill was his son Larry, who was cleaning out the box as the drill rolled along. Behind the drill and Larry was a two-ton, hard-rubber-tire roller that pressed the soil against the seed. As the turn was being made, Larry checked the fertilizer pump, leaning forward. With the drill turned around, Ivan lowered it. The row marker fell into the soil, and the tractor and equipment surged ahead.

Once everything was headed in the right direction, Ivan glanced back to see how the equipment was doing. To his surprise, Larry was nowhere to be seen!

Coming to a quick stop, Ivan ran back to see what had happened. His heart almost stopped; Larry was lying motionless, face down, about 25 feet behind the roller, pressed almost flat into the soil.

Praying for strength to accept what he would find, Ivan hurried to his son's side. Before too long, the dirty form began to move, a groan escaping his lips.

"Where am I? What happened?" Larry asked, confused. For Ivan, the sound of his son's voice was the sound of music.

Ivan explained that the roller had run over him, but Larry did not seem to think that was possible. He asked several more times, "What happened?" For Ivan, seeing his son alive after being smashed by a two-ton roller didn't seem possible!

The roller was in two sections, so the full two tons would not have pressed him. However, from all appearances, his head did *not* line up with the four-inch gap between the sections.

Regaining more of his senses, Larry looked around for his glasses. A quick search found them neatly folded next to his cap, about five

The roller that went over Larry was similar to this one but in two sections.

feet behind him. The glasses were not even broken!

Ivan's wife soon arrived to take Larry to the hospital for a checkup. Nothing appeared to be broken in his body, though he did suffer a concussion that needed time to heal.

Analyzing the situation, they concluded that the row marker had hit Larry on the head as it went down, knocking him unconscious. A gash on his head was the evidence that pointed to the marker as the culprit, though Larry did not remember getting hit.

Larry has not suffered any lasting effects from the incident, but the family feels that God protected him from an accident that could easily have been a lot worse.

Skid-Steer Monsters

How would you look at driving a skid-steer loader if it was called a man-eating monster? But how could you do that when they are such handy tools to have around, both on the farm and on the jobsite? As one dairy farmer commented half-jokingly to me recently, "I don't know how anyone can farm without a skid steer."

Without a doubt, they are versatile, efficient, and labor-saving machines, yet when are we going to quit hearing stories of "So-and-so lost his son in a skid-steer accident"? Maybe if we viewed these tools as man-eaters, we would be more careful when we used them.

How much farther back is safe?

The National Institute of Safety and Health found that about four out of every five skid-steer deaths involved someone getting pinched between the bucket and the frame.[13] Older machines may not have safety features that lock the hydraulics when the machine is turned off or when the safety bar is lifted. But with any machine, one should never fully trust the hydraulic lock when working on a machine. One broken fitting or burst hose and the bucket could fall with a crash.

The next greatest cause of skid-steer deaths is someone getting run over. Skid-steer operators know how difficult it is to see what is behind them, and side vision is also limited. Check out the back of a skid steer sometime. The multitude of scratches on many of them are evidence that they have often backed into objects the operator didn't intend to hit. Here a simple safety rule applies: *Anyone not directly involved in the task should not be allowed into the work area.* Small children in the work area are an absolute no-no when operating a skid steer. They do not realize how hard it is for the operator to see them, especially when backing up.

Keep the safety features in good working condition and resist the temptation to bypass them. Shall I tell you of the young man who is now missing half his foot because a small safety feature on a skid steer wasn't functioning properly? Which would have been cheaper, the $200,000 hospital bill or the $30 part that would have kept the bucket from dropping when the safety bar was raised?

Keep that bucket as low as possible! I remember years ago, when skid steers were relatively new, seeing a co-worker tipped forward, unable to get out of the machine. Another co-worker was laughing as he ran for his camera to get a picture of the dilemma. Suffice it to say, the operator was not the happiest man around to have someone making fun of his failure! But it was his own fault; all he had to do was keep the bucket down while transporting material across the worksite.

My early training in skid-steer operation included an important point: *If the machine starts bucking, let go of the handles.* Too often the operator overcorrects when the machine begins to tip. Then, to correct the overcorrection, he overcorrects the other way. This is known as bucking. The best remedy for this situation is to *let go of the handles.* Most of the time the machine will settle back on all wheels by itself, even if it does hit the ground a bit hard while doing so.

How old does a child need to be to operate a skid steer? There is no set answer that fits every situation, but there is a lot more to operating a machine than knowing what lever does what. Maybe Johnny can reach the pedals at seven years of age and knows how to operate it, but that does not mean he is qualified to run a skid steer.

Finally, and you may get tired of hearing this, but *no riders!* Our communities experience too many runovers by skid steers. One of the worst machines for riders, they are simply not designed for two people in the cab. And they tip and bounce too easily for people to stand in the bucket or jump onto the back. Again I ask, how many more sordid stories of runovers will take place before we simply quit allowing riders on skid steers?

Remember, a skid steer is a handy machine, but it can easily turn into a monster that can paralyze or kill someone.

When Can Johnny Drive the Tractor?

Dad looked at me and asked, "Mike, do you think you could drive the tractor?"

Oh! Only a farm boy of about eight years old can know the thrill of those words! Dad was a well driller as well as a farmer. Drilling by day, he tended the farm in the evenings. But that day the field beside the house needed to be plowed, and he simply didn't have time. Several of us were standing in the field, with the tractor nearby, when the possibility of my doing the plowing came to Dad's mind. I had driven the tractor before, but not a whole lot. Now Dad was giving me the chance to plow a ten-acre field!

"Well," I responded, "I can probably do all right except when it comes to turning around at the end." That was supposed to be a reply of, "Yes, I can do it!" Somehow, though, Dad saw my hesitancy and on second thought decided not to let his eight-year-old boy plow the field.

That disappointment was one of the bigger ones of my childhood, but I got over it. And today I realize that Dad was right. I really wasn't ready to be turned out into a field with a tractor.

Just when is a boy big enough to drive and handle power equipment? No straightforward answer can be given; there are too many variables. Is the boy mentally mature enough to handle the situation if things go wrong? Is he physically large enough to reach the controls? Is he emotionally mature enough not to show off or do something foolish? And of course, included in the equation is whether the civil authorities permit it.

Consider the following safety considerations before allowing a child to operate a piece of power equipment:

- A 12-year-old's reaction time is markedly slower than that of a 15- to 17-year-old.

- Simultaneous motor skills (the ability to do two things at the same time with the arms and the legs) continue to develop between the ages of 14 and 17.

- While a child may safely be able to operate a piece of power equipment under normal circumstances—as I probably could have driven the tractor that day—he may not be able to handle abnormal conditions, such as a hole in the field, a breakdown of equipment, or a dog getting in the way.

- Boys operating equipment may be severely tempted to show off if one of their friends or a sibling shows up. Is he mature enough to resist the temptation?
- Beyond personal safety, is the child old enough to understand the gauges and keep the machine from overheating, running out of oil, etc.?

It Didn't Stop!

Jeffrey, Mark, and Leroy, ages 8 to 13, jumped on their neighbor's New Holland tractor to bring it to their chicken house. The tractor was in the 35-horsepower range, with a hydrostatic transmission. Mark did the driving, while Jeffrey, who was oldest, stood on the right floorboard. Leroy, the youngest of the trio, took his place on the left floorboard.

Cruising up to the door of the chicken house, Mark released his foot from the forward pedal . . . but the tractor kept going! Unbeknownst to any of them, Jeffrey's foot was under the reverse pedal, preventing the forward pedal from disengaging. With a crash, bang, and clang, the tractor surged through the sliding metal door. The door swung into the chicken house when the front of the tractor pushed it in. From there, the rollover protection bar caught the door and safely lifted it over the heads of the boys.

As the tractor entered the barn, Jeffrey bailed off, leaving his boot under the reverse pedal. As he fell to the concrete floor, the rear wheel of the tractor ran over his leg. Mark, gripped with fear, slammed his foot on both brake pedals, causing the tractor to stall.

Other than a sore ankle from the tractor running over Jeffrey's foot, the boys walked away without any physical harm. Had the rollover protection system not been in place, the ripped sheet metal of the door could easily have severely injured the boys. The incident put a fear in Jeffrey's heart for several years about using tractors and equipment. The lesson they learned was clear: *No riders on farm equipment!*

The chicken house where the accident occurred—with new siding!

Just a Little Hydraulic Oil

It was just a little oil, but it was in the wrong place. The effects of it were best described as gruesome.

That misplaced oil may have amounted to only a few drops, but those drops were shot into someone's finger at up to 3,000 psi. Picture a hydraulic hose that has a pinhole, shooting out a stream of oil so fine you may not even be able to see it. All you see is an oily area, indicating a leak. As you feel over the line with your hand to check for leaks, you feel something like a pinprick. It may make you jerk your hand away. But when you look at your hand, you see only a tiny little spot that looks like a wire prick. *Did the hose have a wire sticking out?* you wonder.

So you go on with life, ignoring a little pain. But after only a few hours, the area around the pinprick starts throbbing and turning red. By the next day, some of it is turning black and blue, and the throbbing is getting worse. You finally go see the doctor. The doctor tells you the horrible news. It can be distilled to one word: amputation.

Yes, many men have lost a finger, a hand, an arm, or even a leg to just a little bit of injected hydraulic oil. The oil is under extreme pressure and pushes deep into the skin, and even into the muscles. Once there, infection can set in. If it is not dealt with quickly, gangrene can set in, which may require an amputation. If this seems like an exaggeration, do an internet search and see if you still think so.

There are ways to avoid getting an oil injection while searching for a hydraulic leak. Find a piece of paper, cardboard, or Plexiglas. Pass this material over the hose rather than your finger, and watch for oil on the material. Be aware that the pressure can cut right through paper materials, so you should still keep your hands away from the hoses. Again, the leak may be too small to see with the eye, but the pressure can be up to 3,000 psi on some systems and can literally cut through your skin.

Besides getting an injection, the oil in hydraulic systems is often hot—hot enough to cause burns. This is another reason to use paper or cardboard to check for leaks.

To prevent an oil injection into your fingers, use paper to check for the source of a hydraulic oil leak.

Except for some diagnostic purposes, always turn off the machine while you are servicing or working on a hydraulic system. Remember that when you crack a fitting open, the pressure in the system may drain out and a hydraulic cylinder may suddenly release its load. Too many lives have been lost and too many men crippled because of equipment dropping while a hydraulic system was being serviced.

Getting pinched is not the only danger. People can get soaked with hot hydraulic oil when a hydraulic fitting bursts open. Remember the previous warning about being burned by drops of hot oil? Imagine a quart of hot hydraulic oil being poured over your body!

While on the subject of oil injection, let's review some other possible injection possibilities. Air compressors can shoot air into the blood stream. If this goes to the brain, it can cause a stroke.

Paint sprayers are another injection hazard, with oil-based paints and thinners being particularly dangerous if injected. Like oil injections and other high-pressure injections, the amputation rate can be high, especially if a person is not treated within a few hours.[14]

Some diesel engine fuel lines are also under high pressure. Again, use a piece of material to find the leak, rather than running your fingers over the lines.

And of course, we all know that pressure washers shoot out water at extremely high pressure. Since the volume is higher, the ejected water is less likely to inflict injury, and water is less toxic than oils. But water shooting out at 2,000 psi is far from being a simple shower. I have seen people using a pressure washer to cut open a watermelon and cut through a leather shoe. How much would it take to cut a person open?

Tractor Rollovers

As a boy growing up on a farm in Indiana, we laughed and laughed at the older man from West Virginia who once told us that he knew of a mule that fell out of the garden and broke its leg. Fall *out* of a garden? What kind of hillbilly tale was that? Mules might fall down *in* a garden, but fall *out* of one?

If the gentleman who told us the story had not been a sincere Christian, we Hoosier farm boys would most likely have written it off as a tall tale, and we nearly did so anyway. Then one day we loaded up as a family to go to a church meeting in eastern West Virginia. I suppose those West Virginians could have snickered at us flatlanders as we gaped at the steep mountains while driving down the highway. Yes, we could now see that in West Virginia it was indeed possible for a mule to fall *out* of a garden!

That same eye-opening recognition of a world bigger than flat farmlands came over me concerning tractor rollovers. Our farm in Indiana did have a couple of small hills, and once my dad had rolled a small riding lawnmower on a steep little hill in the yard. But rollover protection structure (ROPS) made little sense to me. I did not know of a single person who had rolled a tractor in his fields. So when the government began to urge tractor manufacturers to install a ROPS on all new tractors, it seemed like government over-regulation. I am pretty sure that had we bought a tractor with a ROPS, one of the first things we would have done was remove it.

But just like the revelation of mules falling out of a garden, tractor rollovers became a personal reality to me when I moved to Greene County, Pennsylvania. There, in the southwestern corner of Pennsylvania, right next to West Virginia, I found many people who had experienced a rollover with a tractor. In fact, if a person living in Greene County had not rolled a tractor, he almost certainly knew someone who had. Just about every farmer in the area could tell a rollover tale, either about his neighbor or himself. ROPS suddenly made perfect sense!

The data

How often does a tractor get rolled? Data from the United States indicates that one out of every ten tractor operators will end up rolling a tractor during his lifetime. About 130 people die yearly in tractor rollovers, meaning one death in a little less than every three days. Tractor rollovers are the leading cause of farm deaths in the United States. Many tractor rollovers cause death, while others produce severe injuries.[15]

A few simple safety guidelines will help you avoid being one of those 130 people who die every year because of a tractor rollover.

- Always use a seat belt in conjunction with a ROPS. If both a seat belt and a ROPS are used together, fatalities in rollovers drop 99 percent. If ROPS is used but no seat belt, fatalities only drop by 70 percent.[16]
- Do not use tractors on slopes of more than 20 percent (11°). While most farmers may use them on slopes greater than that without incident, keeping this in mind will put the operator in a "safety mode" mentality if using a tractor on hills. On steep slopes, drive up and down the hill rather than sideways.
- When driving on slopes, remember that a hole, such as a groundhog hole,

can cause a rollover. A sharp turn can also throw the tractor over on a hillside.

- Some ROPS come with a folding option, useful in low-clearance areas. Remember to unfold the ROPS when you finish working in a low-clearance area.

- Homemade ROPS are not recommended as many of them lack the strength needed in crucial moments. Also, the factory-built ROPS should not be modified as this could decrease their ability to stand up in a rollover.

- If a tractor with a ROPS does roll over, the ROPS should be replaced. The system may have been compromised and may not hold up the next time.

- It does not take a long hill to produce a rollover. A quick online search for tractor rollovers shows many tractors on their side or upside down after rolling on a little bank or ditch. Sometimes rollovers happen in flatland states. You do not need to live in West Virginia to roll a tractor.

- Not only can a tractor roll over sideways, in the right conditions they can also roll over backwards. With the earliest tractors, many men were killed when their plow hit a snag and the tractor reared up and flipped over backwards.

- Use extra caution when using older tricycle front-end tractors, as they are more prone to a rollover than wide front-end tractors.

- Do not pull something with the ROPS. This could weaken the system and cause it to fail in a moment of crisis.

This happened to the photographer's grandfather. Fortunately, he only got bruised. The cab probably saved his life. Note that the bank where the tractor flipped is not very steep. Did Grandpa hit an unseen hole? This tractor is a foreign version of a Massey Ferguson. Even our favorite model can roll over!

Prepare to Meet Thy God . . . While Plowing

One of my plowing experiences involved a 1586 International Harvester tractor with a six-bottom plow. I was working for my mother's first cousin as the plowboy on his large farming operation in Indiana. Being the plowboy meant I was responsible for plowing up to 1,200 acres in the fall after the crops were harvested, though sometimes I was not the only one plowing. Needless to say, I spent a lot of hours in the seat of a tractor.

For the most part, the ground in that part of the state was level and not rocky. This meant that plowing was usually uneventful, with the fields being anywhere from a few hundred feet long to almost a mile.

The longest field also had a high area of hard clay, so in that area the tractor had to pull a little harder. At first this didn't seem to be much of a problem, and shifting down a gear took care of the issue. Until . . . all of a sudden, I found myself staring straight ahead at the top of the front wheels, which were normally below my line of sight! Yes, the front end was rising, with the wheels appearing to be about three feet off the ground.

I did what all novice plowboys are likely to do in such an instance: I hit the clutch as fast as I could, in panic. *BAM!* The front wheels hit the ground with a jar. I realized instantly that hitting the clutch was probably not the best thing to do, but this was my first experience with a rising front end. After a few more trials and errors, I learned that with a low gear and a careful maneuver of the throttle I could make the tractor pull through that tough spot with the front end off the ground a little. I also raised the plow a little so it could move through the clay more easily. Once the tractor had passed the clay, the front end would usually settle back down easily without jarring.

Had I been plowing sixty years earlier, I may not have lived to write this story. The early Fordson tractors had a reputation as killers. One person even claimed that Ford Motor Company should have painted "Prepare to meet thy God" on the hoods of their Fordson tractors. Many farmers lost their lives when pulling a plow with their Fordson tractors. After the plow hit a snag, rock, or other hard place, the Fordson stopped moving forward. The force would then flip the tractor over backwards, often killing the operator.

Perhaps the issue was, as Ford Motor Company complained, a lack of operator skill and wisdom. But around 100 men a year were killed by tractor flip-overs in the late 1910s and early 1920s, and not that many farmers were using tractors at the time. It is easy to see why the tractors got a reputation as men-killers.

The problem was also that those early tractors were all using pull-type plows. Part of the sales pitch for the later 3-point hitch equipment is that they prevented flip-overs.

Do people still flip tractors over backwards? Absolutely! Recently I saw a video of a man flipping a tractor over while trying to pull a pickup out of the mud. The truck was stuck too deep to budge and when the tractor wheels caught traction, the tractor flipped over within a second or two. Safety experts say a tractor can flip backwards in one and a half seconds, with the point of no return being reached in only three-quarters of a second.[17] Thankfully, the operator in the video survived because the tractor turned slightly as it went over. A ROPS would also have helped in that particular incident.

The lesson

When using a chain while pulling with a tractor, always hitch the chain as low as possible on the back of the tractor. If the chain is hooked to a point higher than the axle, the natural force of the pull will tend to lift the front end off the ground. Hooking lower does not guarantee that the front end will not rise and eventually flip over, but it will help.

This old photo had no explanation as to why the tractor rolled. I suspect it flipped over and rolled when the plow snagged something.

The above point is doubly important when pulling uphill. A load that would pull fine on level ground may be enough to flip the tractor when on an incline.

PTOs—<u>P</u>eople-<u>T</u>angling <u>O</u>bjects

Not all memories from long ago are good memories. Younger generations are blessed not to have the memory of PTO shafts without guards. Perhaps such a PTO could stand for *<u>p</u>eople-<u>t</u>angling <u>o</u>bject* instead of *<u>p</u>ower <u>t</u>ake-<u>o</u>ff*.

Although a PTO shaft has no mind of its own, perhaps we would respect it more if we saw it as watching and waiting for the opportunity to grab our clothing and shout victory every time it managed to do so.

Do these people-tangling objects win sometimes? Of course! An arm torn out of its socket, a leg with damaged muscles, both legs amputated below the knees, head injuries, and even death have been the result of getting tangled in a PTO shaft. All it takes is a loose piece of clothing, a shredded coattail, a shoestring, or a long beard or hair, and it's too late to turn off the power. Sadly, in many cases the PTO will win the tug-of-war.

At 540 rpm, a PTO shaft spins 9 times per second. At 1,000 rpm, it whirls along at 16.6 times a second. Do we really think we can move faster than that? Even at idling speeds, the shaft can turn at two times per second. That means that when you lift your leg to step over the shaft and happen to notice that your shoestring passes right into the universal joint of the shaft, you have about one-fourth second to yank it out before the shaft makes that half turn to start tangling. And once it starts the wrap, you are done. You may end up with your shoes and your pants ripped off and your leg muscles severely damaged within a couple of seconds, as happened in a recent incident. Or maybe the PTO will just snap your shoestring and life will hurry on. Do you really want to take the gamble?

That is why you should never step over a spinning PTO shaft. I know, you are in a hurry. (Hurrying is the context of many accidents, right?) To walk all the way around the tractor or implement would take up precious time and you're tempted to just step over the PTO. *Don't do it!* Not even with a shaft guard in place. Bad habits make for bad results down the line.

Always turn off the PTO before dismounting a tractor unless it is necessary to keep the implement running (like a silage blower). Occasionally a baler or other implement

Does this PTO shaft represent farm equipment on a typical U.S. farm? In this case, the rough plastic driveline shield may pose a greater danger than no shield.

may need to be running to diagnose a problem. But in general, *shut off the PTO when you dismount a tractor.*

Keep guards in place. Older tractors may have had the PTO master shield removed, but the shields were put there for a purpose, and replacing a missing one may save an arm or leg—or a life. A small percentage of PTO accidents involve getting tangled in the PTO stub on the tractor when no shaft is attached. The master shield makes a nice step on some tractors. But remember that if the shaft is spinning and your pant leg is a typical farmer pant leg (with shreds hanging down), you are tempting the *people-tangling object* to grab ahold for a game of tug-of-war. And remember, PTO shafts usually win these battles.

When repairing PTO shafts, do not use long bolts at the couplings or replace shear pins with longer ones than the original. Any spinning bolt head or tail adds to the tangling danger.

Regularly check the bearings on the driveline shield (the smooth plastic or metal cover around the shaft, with belled ends over the universal joints). Sometimes plastic ones burst, and the sharp edges are just waiting to grab hold of some shirttail and give it a spin. If the driveline shield comes with a tether, use it. An untethered shield is supposed to stop spinning when it is held or when it tangles with something, but the shield can become locked to the shaft and continue spinning when a shirttail gets tangled into it. The tether is to show that the shield is indeed running freely from the shaft.

Finally, when working around these *people-tangling objects,* keep your clothes tight against you, your long hair or beard in place, and your shoelaces where they belong. One man whose loose shirt blew into the PTO lost his right foot when it was all said and done.

The history of this five-decade-old tractor seems to include the removal of the PTO master shield. (Did you notice the four threaded bolt holes around the top part of the stub?) Whose shoelace will be the next to get into a tug-of-war with this PTO stub? Put on a new shield!

Praises in the Woods

Being a jack-of-all-trades, my work experiences have varied from construction to farming to writing books to woodworking . . . and even to sawmilling and logging. Of all my work experiences, I give logging the dubious honor of being the most dangerous. Even though it has been some years—actually decades—since I earned my living by tipping lodgepole pines in Montana, I recall how I sometimes stopped, took off my hardhat, bowed my head, and sincerely thanked God for protecting me from a tree that did not go where I had wanted it to go.

Oh, the messes I got myself into! Around 90 percent of the trees went where I had planned. But when you cut one hundred trees in a day, that averages out to ten trees a day that fall in a different direction than intended. A 20-degree change in direction may not seem so bad, but it may mean that the tree gets hung up in another tree instead of neatly falling into the open space where it was supposed to go.

One way to remedy a hung-tree situation is to cut a second tree and drop it onto the first one. Sometimes this smashed down the hung-up tree, but sometimes you ended up with two hung-up trees, or even three or four.

Thankfully, loggers today are more safety conscious than those of a century ago. Notice the man at the top who is topping the tree. It doesn't look very safe at the bottom either!

Finally the realization dawns that the only way out of the mess is to cut the tree that is trapping the other trees. Since I was supposed to be harvesting only the dead trees, cutting a green tree was officially a no-no, although the Forest Service permitted taking out an occasional live tree "under necessity." This was certainly one of those times. The problem was, of course, that several other trees were leaning on the one that needed cutting.

In those situations, the hardhat did not come off to offer up prayers of praise as much as desperate prayers for wisdom and safety! Thankfully, I survived these difficult situations, and you can be sure that when all the trees were safely down on the ground, the prayers for wisdom turned into genuinely heartfelt prayers of praise and thanksgiving!

Dangerous tool

But trees falling the wrong direction, or kicking back while falling, or bouncing when landing, are not the only dangers of logging. Many a person has been injured by the tool used to cut down the tree. In fact, an average day in the United States sees 75 chainsaw accidents, and those are just the ones that are reported.[18]

Cuts are a part of life with a number of professions, but cuts inflicted by chainsaws are different. They rip, tear, and shred. The average chainsaw injury requires 110 stitches to patch up.[19] Some of them are beyond patching, and the recipient needs to go to the undertaker rather than the doctor.

About one-third of chainsaw injuries are to the user's legs or knees. Cut-resistant chaps or pants may be expensive and hot to wear in summer weather, but they beat getting 110 stitches and lying around for a few weeks until your cut heals.

Do not forget good shoes that are made of cut-resistant material. When working with logs and branches, steel-toed boots may save you from toe surgery. Meanwhile, keep the top part of your body safe by wearing a hardhat when working where falling limbs may be present. A good pair of gloves can help keep down scratches and pokes from thorns and briars when handling the saw.

Eye protection is always recommended when using a chainsaw. A face shield will not only guard against flying sawdust, but also protect your precious eyes from whipping branches. Most logging helmets use a mesh face shield, as the plastic ones tend to fog up from the user's breath. The plastic ones offer slightly better protection, however.

And now, listen closely: *Never use a chain saw without hearing protection!* A hearing specialist told me that chainsaws are probably the number one culprit for hearing loss in men who work with machinery. Yes, new chainsaws usually come with a decent muffler, but how long does that muffler stay decent? One year? Two? All too often, chainsaw owners neglect to replace their saw's muffler, especially when they cannot see any damage from the outside. But just because it is not rusted through does not mean the muffler is in good shape.

Kickback watch

The number one safety issue when using a chainsaw is kickback. More than 25 percent of all chainsaw injuries are the result of kickback. If you don't know what kickback is, or what causes it in a chainsaw, then please do not pick up another chainsaw until you know!

Kickback occurs when the chain on the top half of the tip of the bar catches in the wood and throws the saw upward, or sideways if cutting parallel to the ground. This can cause cuts to a person's face, head, or shoulders—and even the jugular vein.

I have found that I can manhandle a small chainsaw (under 60 cc/3.8 CID). This means that if I am prepared for it, I can force the tip of a chainsaw into a log and apply enough muscular power to keep the bar from flying up. In other words, I am stronger than the saw.

But there is a real problem with this. Notice my caveat, "If I am prepared for it." If we get in the habit of forcing the tip into the wood, overcoming the saw's tendency to catch and kick back, it may someday backfire—or more accurately, kick back—on us. Perhaps we are not paying attention as we should, or we are more unbalanced in our stance than we thought. We go ahead and make the jab, only to find that the bar with a spinning chain is on its way to our face.

I learned one lesson when using a larger chainsaw (96 cc/6.0 CID). As much as I tried, I could simply not hold back that saw from kickback if the tip got into the wood too much. After having been used to manhandling the smaller saws for many years, I found it quite scary.

My point is this: Never develop the habit of manhandling small saws out of kickback. Make it a habit to avoid cutting with the tip. To remind yourself of the danger of kickback, paint your bar like this. Do not use the painted part to initiate a cut.

Miscellaneous chainsaw safety

While kickback and accidentally cutting one's leg make up the majority of chainsaw accidents, other safety issues need our attention as well. Review the following list before heading out to gather up this year's firewood.

- When holding a chainsaw, always wrap your thumb around the handle. This way your hand will stay in place and hit the brake if the saw kicks.

- Study where the tree will fall based on its shape and lean. Don't forget to factor in the wind. And also consider any rot or other defects in the tree.

- Always make sure you have a clear escape route when felling a tree. When the tree starts to lean for the fall, set the saw down and escape the area. The best escape route is often at a 45-degree angle back from the line of desired fall. Of course, make sure the tree is not accidentally falling onto your escape route before exiting. Planning for this escape route may mean cutting brush and clearing out briars.

- Never straddle a tree trunk or limb while cutting it. Unseen pressure may make it kick in any direction.

- Use ropes and cables to guide the fall of trees that do not have a clear direction for the fall.

- Do not use a chainsaw above shoulder height.

- Watch for dead branches that may fall while felling a tree. This is especially important when using wedges, as pounding on the wedge may cause a dead limb to snap off. In the eastern United States, many ash trees have died in recent years. Be aware that although dead ash branches can look solid from the ground, they may break off when the tree starts tipping over.

- Watch for limbs that are under pressure when de-limbing fallen trees.

- When felling trees, always leave a "hinge." Be aware that dead trees need a larger hinge, because when the tree starts falling, the dead wood of the hinge may suddenly snap and the tree is then free to fall in any direction. (That is the voice of experience speaking! I have seen a dead tree start to fall in the intended direction, but then suddenly the hinge snapped and the tree went 90 degrees in the other direction.)

- Always place the saw on the ground to start it. Do not use the "drop start" method, in which the operator holds the starter cord and drops the saw in a jerk. This is dangerous because the operator only has one hand on the saw, making it unstable. It could swing into his leg once started. The correct method is to set the chain brake, set the saw on the ground, put one hand on the top bar and one foot into the handle, and then pull the starter cord.

- Never fuel a hot saw, and move the saw away from the refueling spot before starting. This will guard against igniting any spilled fuel.

- Use a case during transportation, and preferably do not transport a chainsaw inside the passenger compartment of a vehicle.

- Keeping the chain sharp and properly tensioned deters accidents. A dull saw will require much more operator pressure.

Which chainsaw starting method do you use? In the picture on the left, if the saw roars to life, the saw is not stabilized and may swing into the user's leg. In the second picture, the saw is firmly held with an arm and a foot. Note that in both pictures the thumb is wrapped around the handle. This wraparound grip is a must when handling a chainsaw.

Watching Out for Those with Disabilities

It was October 1697 in an eastern valley of France near the village of La Petite Liepvre. Several Amish men were cleaning up a field on one of the hillsides. One of them, Hans Weiss, finished toppling over a tree only to see the log go rolling down the hill straight toward Peter Zimmerman. The problem was, Peter could not hear the log coming. It is not known if Hans yelled or not, but it would not have helped, as Peter was deaf. Despite this disability, Peter was an ordained minister and the owner of a sawmill.

The log hit Peter, seriously injuring him. Not long after, he died from the injuries. The community quickly arranged a funeral and buried Peter's body alongside a row of trees.

In those days, it may not have been required to report such an accident to the civil authorities, and apparently this incident was not reported. However, when the local authorities got wind of it, they exhumed the body and made an investigation, probably wondering if foul play was involved. The local Amish bishop, the famed Jakob Ammann, and several family members all testified to the authorities what had happened, and the case was settled. Everyone had forgiven poor Hans Weiss.

What can we learn from this accident?

- Today's large equipment increases the risk for accidents in some ways, but even simpler times saw tragedies. It doesn't take a $500,000 log skidder to kill someone while logging!

- People with disabilities should not be excluded from taking their part in society, but extra care needs to be taken when working with them. For example, since Peter Zimmerman was deaf, those working for him and around him should have added that to their safety thinking. Perhaps we are working

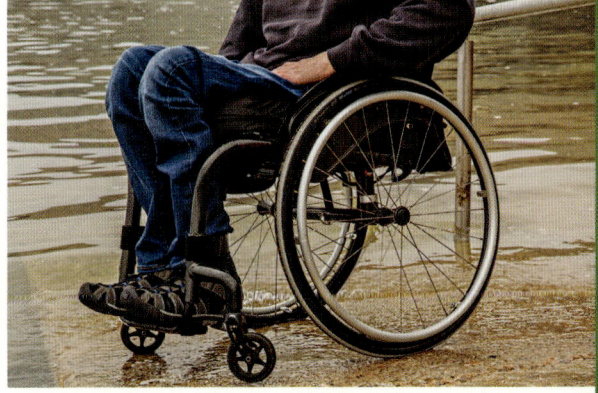

While this man may be limited in what he can physically do on a project, his mental capabilities and experience could be invaluable. Those on the site need to keep in mind, however, that it might take him a little longer to get out of harm's way.

around individuals who are mentally handicapped. Though they may be doing jobs that fit their capabilities, their response to dangerous situations may not be as fast as that of the average person.

- When accidents do occur, the civil authorities should be notified if that is what is required. They will be less likely to press charges if the incident is reported than if it is covered up and they find out through rumor. Christians should be leaders in practicing safety. If the civil authorities see us taking steps to teach and practice safety, they will be less likely to penalize us when something does happen. But if Christians are the worst slackers, then the authorities may be inclined to lay on the penalties when an accident occurs.

Shop and Construction Safety

Why You Don't Read Safety Warnings

Imagine my surprise—and amusement—when I saw a graphic similar to the following one on the "Instructions and Safety Warnings" that came with a pack of finish nails from a major tool manufacturer.

Well, whatever! Who doesn't know that you are not supposed to put your nail gun on the head of your helper? Over the next few days I had more than one chuckle over this graphic. *This is exactly why people often don't read safety warnings,* I found myself thinking. *They can be so ridiculous!*

From there, I became a bit sarcastic, finally concluding that the caption for the graphic could read, "WARNING! Choose your work partners carefully, because there are some real dunces out there who will rest their nail gun on your head!"

During this time, I showed the warning to a friend, and he told me of someone from a Plain community who had deactivated the safety mechanism on his nail gun so he could shoot nails faster. One day a co-worker coming up a ladder hit the tip of the nail gun with his head, and the gun fired a nail into his head. The victim survived but not without a medical ordeal.

Now let's go back and look at a summary of the original caption: "Do not keep your finger on the trigger of a nailer."

The point of the graphic is that the man with the gun has his finger on the trigger. A co-worker, maybe his son, is below him and could stand up at any time. Since Dad's finger is on the trigger, as soon as that happens, *BANG!* . . . a nail goes into the son's head.

Is that a stupid warning? Not at all. Here are the lessons to remember:

- Keep your finger off the trigger of a nailer unless you are planning to drive in a nail.
- Do not deactivate the safety mechanisms on equipment.
- Read the safety warnings that come with tools and equipment; they are there to remind us of common sense.
- Be careful with sarcasm about safety!

Knot in the Eye

Ripping a board on a table saw was nothing new to 23-year-old Ervin. Having grown up in his father's mini-barn business, he had been using power tools for a number of years. One morning Ervin grabbed a 2x6 board and turned on the saw to rip the board into two pieces.

Normally Ervin wore eye protection when using the table saw, as his father had urged him to do. But for this one quick rip, he decided to forgo the usual precaution.

As the blade neatly sliced the board, Ervin suddenly felt a pain in his eye. A loose knot had been thrown by the blade and had hit him squarely in the right eye! The knot appears to have been traveling so fast that Ervin didn't even have time to blink, as later inspection revealed that the eyelid was not damaged at all.

Ervin's father contacted their local eye doctor, who informed them that the situation was too serious for them to deal with. He recommended an ophthalmologist, who found that the knot had hit Ervin squarely in the eyeball and that it needed to be sewn up. Using a technique to dry the eyeball and shrink it so that it could be removed from the socket, the eyeball was sewn up and then put back into the socket. Then the normal moisture was put back in.

The doctors gave Ervin a 50 percent chance that the eye would perform normally. Today, with a special +11 contact lens in the damaged eye, he can make out large print or recognize someone across the room. Nine years after the accident Ervin needed surgery to correct a detached retina, probably because of the previous trauma.

Now let's consider this from another angle. The original repair to the eye cost around $6,000. When the retina detached, the family received an 80 percent self-pay discount but still had to spend another $10,000. Suppose Ervin spent even five minutes to hunt down a pair of safety glasses. Those five minutes would have saved $16,000, plus a lifetime of poor sight. Is it any wonder that Ervin encourages everyone to take care of the gift of eyesight God has given us?

Almost launched!

We do not always think of table saws as extremely dangerous to the eyes, but Ervin's case goes to show that any fast-moving tool has the potential to fling objects into the eyes. And fling them faster than what you can blink!

As I was writing this book, I was working at remodeling an old house. During the process, I used a miter saw. I assumed it would not be necessary to use safety glasses since the blade in a miter saw pushes the sawdust and debris *away* from the user as it cuts. Just days after getting Ervin's story, I cut a board with a miter saw. Imagine my feelings when the blade quit spinning and I saw the scene in the photo.

Where would that knot have gone had it dislodged? Sure, the blade was pushing it away from my eyes, but what if it had hit the guard after dislodging? Where could it have gone from there?

Sobering knot, not?

Always wear safety glasses when operating any power saw!

Hastening to Cut Off His Thumb

Paul practically grew up in his father's woodworking shop. As he matured, he was slowly given permission to use some of the tools. Eventually he was allowed to use the bandsaw.

One of Paul's hobbies was to cut out wooden toys. As he was stacking wood one day behind the large belt sander, the belt tore. Seeing that there would be a little time before the belt was repaired, he hurried to the bandsaw to finish cutting out a scope for a wooden gun he was making for his brother. If he hurried, maybe he could finish it before he was needed back at the belt sander.

"Haste makes waste," the saying goes. This time, hastening through the job, Paul ended up almost losing his thumb. Just as he finished making the last part of a cut, the piece shot through the bandsaw's blade . . . with his thumb going along—right into the blade!

His scream was heard even by a neighbor lady. The pain was worse than anything Paul had ever before experienced. Grabbing his thumb with his other hand, he was relieved to see that it was still attached, although it was bloody and cut deeply. When his father saw it, he quickly decided this was a case for a doctor to handle.

The doctor discovered that the blade had cut two nerves, severed the flexor tendon, and even nicked the bone. It wouldn't have taken too much more, and the thumb would have come completely off.

Recovery was not nearly as hasty as the cutting. First they sewed the thumb up temporarily, then a week later it was time for real surgery. After two hours of surgery, Paul emerged with the damaged thumb repaired as well as the doctors could do. The recovery period was filled with burning and tingling. Bike riding, running, and even schoolwork were off-limits for a while. Paul needed help to do many basic things he normally did for himself. This was humbling, of course, but it was part of the lesson that "haste makes waste"! Not only was time wasted, thousands of dollars were required to pay for the medical expenses. All for just a few seconds of hurried cutting.

Not so precious memories . . .

The photos on the next page show some of the memories that will follow Paul for the rest of his life. Although it was a great learning experience, Paul would probably tell you that he would have preferred to have learned this lesson some other way!

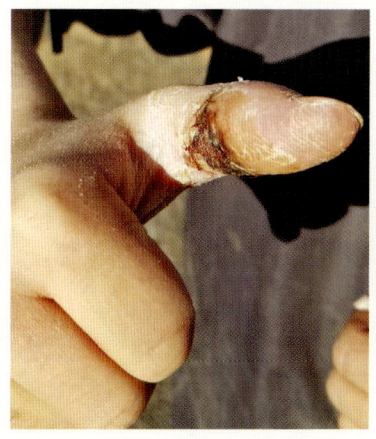 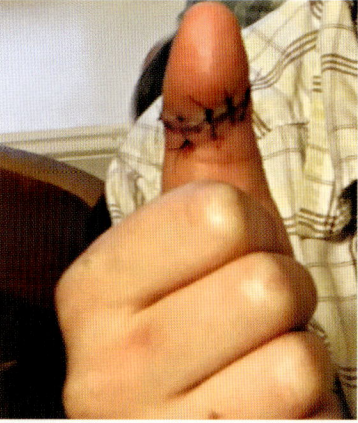 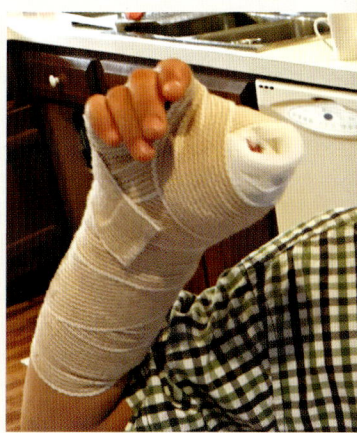

A Safer Table Saw

Every source I consulted about woodshop safety tells the same story—no tool in the shop outdoes the table saw in taking off human fingers. Of the many dangerous woodworking tools in a typical woodworking shop in the United States, 42 percent of the injuries occur while using a table saw.[20] While kickbacks and flung chips or knots cause some of the injuries, most of the damage is old-fashioned cuts. With a blade that typically turns at 3,450 rpms, and an average of 40 teeth on that blade, that equals a cutting tooth coming along every 1/2300 of a second.

With that in mind, let's talk about the reality of what is going to happen if your finger gets into the blade for just half a second. In that half second, your finger will get chewed 1,150 times by a sharp tooth. Is it any wonder why the saw *always* wins in a tooth vs. finger combat?

An average of 11 people in the United States have to suffer through an amputation every single day because of an accident involving a table saw. Those are just the amputations; the total annual U.S. table saw injuries of all types are 67,000. And remember, this does not include the injuries that are not reported at medical centers. And the dollar figure for those 67,000 injuries? $2,130,000,000. That's right—$2.13 *billion!*

SawStop

In recent years, a forward-thinking engineer has found a way to eliminate 99 percent of all finger cuts on table saws. The blade is given a small electrical charge that is continuously monitored. As soon as the sensor realizes that the electrical charge has been grounded, a brake is applied and the blade instantly drops down. Perhaps you have seen the promotional video for this feature. A hotdog is put into the spinning blade, which causes it to stop instantly—as soon as the hotdog touches the teeth. The result is a tiny nick in the hotdog that would hardly even bleed if it were a finger.

So why not put this astonishing safety mechanism on all table saws? The answer is *money*. New saws with this technology cost about two to four times what a regular saw does. And another thing, when the safety mechanism is tripped, the blade is ruined. With the replacement of a new brake and blade, the costs can be $100 or more every time it is utilized. But would it not be worth all these costs if it meant saving a finger?

A $100 replacement brake and blade seems like a good deal compared to a mangled or missing finger. However, because the electric charge that sets off the brake can also be triggered by wet wood, it could be frustrating to owners to have to shell out $100 just because the wood was wetter than the operator realized and the brake activated unnecessarily.

Going back to that $2.13 billion annual medical cost for cut fingers and hands . . . How many new safe saws could be purchased in a year with that money? The answer: about 1,000,000. That means it would take about 10 years to replace all the current table saws in the United States.

Would it be worth the cost? Probably so, but the issue of people not being able to afford a deluxe saw is no easy obstacle to hurdle. Consider my own little woodshop. If I would have had to wait until I could afford to buy a $2000 table saw, I would not have been able to start woodworking nearly as early in life. As it was, I could buy a smaller used saw for less than $200—about one-tenth the price of a new saw with the safety feature (a used one would be cheaper, of course). It is for this reason, most likely, that the U.S. government has so far refused to make it a law that all new table saws be required to have an electronic braking system, though some people are pushing for that law.

If you can afford it, the extra money for a safer saw may be money saved in the long run. If you doubt that, just ask one of the 4,000 people a year who cut off their finger with a table saw!

For the rest of us

For those of us who cannot afford one of the safer table saws, there are options. These options are common-sense table saw safety practices. Following these will drastically lower the chances of you losing a finger in a table saw. Let's review them.

- Do not reach over the blade to make a cut or retrieve finished pieces. There is a reason this rule is first. *Don't do it!*

- Keep the guards in place. Missing guards contribute to missing fingers.

- Keep the saw and the area around it free of debris. This includes the area you will need to handle long stock. You can carefully watch your hands while ripping a board, but if you trip or slip on debris you may not be able to keep from falling into the spinning blade.

- In addition to keeping the floor clean, make sure you are balanced well as you handle the material.

- Set the blade to no more than one-fourth inch above the thickness of the stock. Setting the blade as low as possible means it will not cut as deeply if you do have an accident.

- Keep out of line for kickback. A relative of mine almost died when a board kicked back out of a large planer and hit him in the stomach. A table saw can also kick back. Ask anyone who has operated one for a while!

- Use push sticks if your fingers get within six inches of the blade. Use a featherboard for smaller rips.

Can't afford an expensive push stick? This one has served me well for around 10 years now. The tape on the handle end is a reminder that it is not a scrap piece of wood to be thrown away. How many times has this piece of "scrap" wood saved my fingers from the saw teeth?

- Get a helper if you are ripping boards longer than your saw platform can keep from tipping. If a helper is unavailable, use rolling stands.

- Do not try sawing "freehand." Use either the fence or the miter gauge to stabilize the stock. Do not use both the fence and the miter gauge together as this could put your stock into a bind.

- Do not wear gloves while operating a table saw. They will not allow you to feel the wood as well, and loose gloves may drag you into the blade. Do not wear loose, hanging clothing while operating a table saw.

- Wear eye and hearing protection while sawing.

- Never adjust the saw while it is running.

- Keep the table of the saw clean from rust so that stock can slide over it smoothly and evenly.

- Check the stock for hardware and loose knots before ripping. A nail or screw in the stock can be flung back into the operator's eye.

Walter's Welding Woes

When I think of welding safety, one story that comes to my mind is about Walter, a friend of mine in high school. Walter was a big, easygoing fellow and had the custom of always wearing bib overalls. Bib overalls were *not* in style in those days, so that gives you a hint of his character.

We were in welding class, and I was standing beside one of the metal lathes when I noticed Walter across the room in one of the welding booths. The reason I noticed him was because the frayed ends of his bib overalls were on fire!

"Walter, your pants are on fire!" a friend and I hollered to him.

Walter was not one to get too excited about anything, but he came to life when he pulled up his welding helmet and looked down at his pants. A slap here and a slap there with his big hands soon extinguished the flames, with the only damage being Walter's embarrassment. I have a memory of him giving us one of his big grins, pulling his welding helmet back down over his face, and getting back to work.

Since the incident happened in a public school, I doubt that the building could have caught fire. The walls were masonry, and school rules would have prohibited having any flammable liquids such as gasoline in the room.

But imagine such a scene happening in certain shops that are in less than good order. Imagine sparks flying under the workbench, and instead of lighting up someone's pant legs, igniting oily rags. And imagine that those sparks smoldered in the rags for twenty minutes before igniting into flames, and the welder had finished his job and left ten minutes before the flames arose.

Fire is indeed one of the biggest concerns when we think of welding safety. Safety organizations recommend that any combustibles be at least 35 feet away when welding. In my own shop, I make it a safety rule never to store gasoline in the shop, even in sealed containers.

But there are plenty of combustibles other than gasoline. Diesel, kerosene, oils, and greases are all waiting for that stray spark from the welder or torch. And what about flammables like paper products and rags? And frayed pant legs like Walter's?

A clean shop is a safer shop. Keep the area around the welder and torch free of any flammables. If the need arises to weld outside of the safe shop setting—and that does happen—inspect the area well before striking the first arc. Old buildings can have dry wood, sawdust, and trash lying around. Straw is even worse.

Once when I was welding, the insides of a vehicle door caught fire in an area I couldn't even see while I was welding. This is why you should stick around at least 30 minutes after welding in any area where the heat could have ignited something.

When thinking of fires in the welding shop, we also need to remind ourselves that acetylene is extremely dangerous. Acetylene burns hotter than any other commercially used gas. It can ignite in a range of conditions from 2.5 to 81 percent air. Being just barely lighter than air, it hangs around and mixes in, meaning that a leaking hose or regulator can fill the air with acetylene and cause a grinder or welder spark to ignite the whole mass.

Fumes

Another major concern with welding safety is that many fumes can be present when welding various metals. Nickel and stainless steel are known for their noxious fumes, with both of them suspected to be carcinogenic (meaning they can potentially cause cancer). Obviously, you will not die from your first whiff of any nickel or stainless-steel welding fumes, but you should avoid breathing them as much as possible. Use ventilation to draw in fresh air if welding in a tight place.

Zinc, cadmium, chromium, copper, fluoride, lead, and manganese can give off fumes that cause metal-fume fever. Various paints and powder coatings can also make a welder sick. Because of the high heat involved in welding operations, be aware that chemical reactions may occur that would not normally be a problem at room temperatures.

Electrical shock

Arc welders produce extremely high amperages. These are not normally dangerous to the person welding because the voltages are low enough that they do not usually produce a shock. However, water can change things quickly, providing a path for the current to flow. This means that if you are wet and standing in water, you may feel a shock while changing the rod of an arc welder.

Despite the fact that you can normally change a welding rod in an arc welder without getting shocked, always treat the rod holder and the ground clamps as if they were charged. Turn off the welder while doing any other work on the piece, such as grinding.

What is more likely to happen than getting an electrical shock is getting burned by the hot end of the electrode or even the ground clamp. You can avoid this by wearing welding gloves. Also wear a wool or leather apron or coat and flame-resistant clothing. Be aware that man-made fabrics such as polyester can melt and burn, so avoid wearing clothing of this material while welding.

Leather high-top shoes are recommended; hot sparks falling down and burning through a skimpy shoe may give you an unwanted dancing lesson!

Welding flash

Protect those eyes! Most adults are aware of the danger of watching a welder without eye protection, but children may not be. The danger is from ultraviolet light, which can give the onlooker a case of photokeratitis (welding flash). Thankfully, most of these cases clear up in a day or so without permanent damage, but a person who welds regularly should not permit the damage to occur repeatedly.

Beyond the damage to the eyes, arc welding radiation can produce burns similar to sunburns.

Equipment inspection

As with all tools, regular inspection of welding equipment is a good safety practice. Hoses, wires, gauges, and protection equipment all need to be in good shape. Use caps on oxygen and welding gases while transporting. Do not drag the cylinders on the ground but rather roll them along or cart them. Replace broken gauges; don't guess how much oxygen or acetylene is coming out of the torch tip.

This photo is an excellent lesson on how NOT to weld safely. How many safety violations can you find?

(Possible answers: No helmet, no gloves, no long sleeves, and sparks going into closed space that may include flammable materials.

K-THUMP!

Have you ever had that wheezy feeling in your gut? The kind of feeling that comes after hearing a jacked vehicle hit the ground with a *K-THUMP?*

My experience with that feeling came while living in Bolivia. My Toyota Land Cruiser had a problem that needed to be fixed. I think it must have been one of the times I was repairing the brakes. I eventually found out that the drums had been turned too many times, making the wheel cylinders pop out if the brakes were hit too hard. Until I found that core problem, I fixed the brakes several times.

In places like Bolivia, a nice garage with a car lift is almost nonexistent. I was making the repairs on the porch of the house we were renting. Actually, it was just a cement slab with no roof over it, but at least it was level, relatively clean, and flat. It was the nicest place around to do vehicle repairs.

Using a hydraulic bottle jack, I lifted the vehicle and started repairs. At some point during the repair, I was walking nearby when I heard that gut-wrenching *K-THUMP!* and saw that somehow the jack had slipped out from under the vehicle. Although jack stands were something I did not have on hand, I probably could have rounded up some chunks of wood to use as stands. Anyway, I learned a lesson that day—a car can fall off a jack faster than you can say *K-THUMP!*

And sometimes it can fall for no apparent reason. No one was touching the vehicle. One second it was there, jacked up; the next second it went *K-THUMP* and was not jacked up. That fast! Thank God I was not underneath when it fell. I now make it a rule to never get under a jacked vehicle if it is not on stands.

The Land Cruiser on the porch where it went *K-THUMP* one day.

Jack safety

- About 5,000 people a year are estimated to receive injuries from jacking situations in the United States.[21] This number does not include those who were killed. Nor does it include those who did not seek medical help.

- Jack safety starts with the safety issue illustrated by the preceding story: *Always use jack stands when working on equipment that is jacked up.* Blocks of wood can be used as a stand but avoid concrete blocks because they can suddenly crumble or split without warning.

- Never crawl under a jacked piece of equipment unless plenty of jack stands are in place. This means one stand for every corner lifted. Hydraulic jacks by themselves are not to be trusted.

- Avoid jacking on rounded surfaces. Sometimes no other options are available; in those cases, use double or triple caution.

- Use wheel chocks to keep the vehicle from rolling when jacked. Set the parking brake if the wheels with the parking brake are still on the ground.

- Know the rating on the jack and respect it.

- In awkward situations, a tilted jack may be necessary—such as the time I was trying to lift a bulldozer after a track slipped off in the middle of a mudhole. In general, though, a tilted jack is a recipe for a crash.

- When the equipment is jacked to the proper height, remove the jack handle if possible. This keeps people from bumping into it or tripping over it.

- As with all equipment, regularly inspect jacks to see if they are in good operating condition. You do not want to find out that you used a bad jack while you are under a sinking piece of equipment (although it should not be sinking if you use a stand!). About 18 percent of jack injuries researched in the United States were the result of a bad jack. If we use that percentage with the first safety point above, that means in the United States about a thousand people a year, about three per day, are injured because of jack failure.[22]

Stretching Your Ladder

Anyone who has worked in construction for much time has probably witnessed a ladder accident. The bottom scoots out on an extension ladder, someone leans over too far on a stepladder, or a siding installer suddenly finds the top of his ladder sliding sideways along the side of the building.

Yes, according to OSHA, falls from ladders are one of the leading causes of occupational deaths and injuries.

We all know the rules, right? Don't stand on the top of a stepladder, stay down at least three rungs on a ladder leaning against a building, and so on. Then why are ladders still one of the leading causes of accidents on construction sites?

I think we all know the answer to that question if we have worked at all in construction. *That last nail needs to go in just about two more inches farther than what I should be reaching. I can reach that rafter if I step up on that top step. This ladder surely will not slip out from under me even though I know the floor is a little slick . . .*

And on we go, making excuses, and most of the time we get by with it. I might as well confess: I have done it too.

So let's review ladder safety. Remember, we already know most of these things, but reviewing them etches them into our minds.

- Maintain a three-point contact while ascending or descending a ladder. This means two feet and one hand, or two hands and one foot, should be on the ladder at any given time when going up or down.

- When using a single ladder or extension ladder, always maintain three feet of ladder above the support point. In other words, if you are using a ladder to get onto a roof, keep three feet of ladder above the point where the ladder touches the roof.

- Do not use the top three rungs on a single or extension ladder that is leaned against a structure. You may be forced to lean too far backwards if you are on the top rungs. If you don't have anything available to hang on to, you may lose your balance.

- Secure any ladder that is not resting on a stable base. This could mean a bottom or top securing system, depending on what works best.

- Do not place a ladder on a barrel, box, sawhorses, or other insecure base.
- The proper distance for a single or extension ladder to be angled out is one-fourth the distance of the support height. In other words, if an extension ladder is leaning against a roof 20 feet above the ground, the bottom of the ladder should be 5 feet from the wall. Or if the top is leaning against a wall 12 feet up, then the bottom of the ladder should be 3 feet out.
- Be careful about electrical shock. This is especially important with aluminum ladders. That entrance cable may be a coated wire, but current may shoot through the ladder if the wire has a crack in the coating or is damaged.

Ladders and electrical wires are never a good mixture. An aluminum ladder is doubly dangerous. One bad spot in the wire coating could mean, literally, a very shocking experience. Use extreme caution when working around wiring.

- Obviously, keep ladder rungs clean and free from mud or debris that will make them slick. Clean shoes are a must as well.
- If leaning sideways while on a ladder, try to keep your belt buckle or belly button inside the side rails. That area of your body is the center of your balance. If you get the center of balance outside the side rails, you are much more likely to lose your balance.

- Inspect ladders regularly and keep them in good repair.

- All new ladders come with a weight rating. Know what it is, and figure in the weight of tools and materials that you may be carrying. A 190-pound man who is wearing a tool belt and carrying a bundle of shingles is overloading a ladder rated at 200 pounds.

- If a ladder is placed in front of a closed door, the door should be locked or a notice should be placed nearby so no one will burst through the door and cause an accident.

- Stay off ladders in windstorms.

Sometimes safety will cost you money. These automatic ladder levelers cost about $150 but are well worth the money for people who use extension ladders regularly. This is much safer—and faster—than trying to block up one leg with some boards. Automatic levelers will solidly set in place just by picking the ladder up and setting it down anywhere. This is not just for safety but convenience as well.

Did You Say Hearing Safety?

"Huh? Speak up! I can't hear you."

"What was that?"

"Can you repeat that?"

If you have ever lived with someone with a hearing impairment, you are probably familiar with these frustrated replies. In the early stages of hearing loss, the person with damaged hearing sometimes thinks everyone else is to blame for talking too softly. In these situations, frustration can easily arise—both from the speaker and the listener.

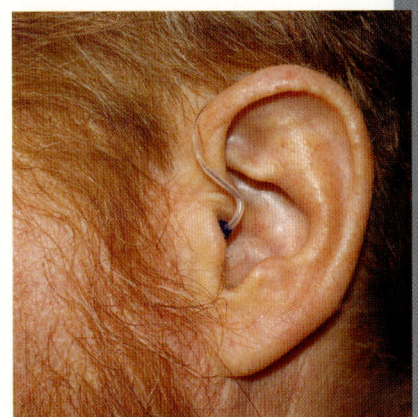

A person with hearing loss may also become withdrawn. In a group conversation, the person may be there physically, but not say much. Some may assume the person with the hearing loss is simply shy, but the real issue is that he or she does not understand all of the conversation. It gets embarrassing to constantly ask others to speak up or repeat what they said, so the person with the hearing loss just pretends—sometimes subconsciously—to be part of the group conversation.

This particular aspect of safety is very personal to me. Let me tell you my story:

When I was in my early 20s, my younger brother bought a digital voltage/ohm meter. Since we had been used to analog meters with a needle, a digital one was a novelty. As I sat in the dining room tinkering with it, my brother in the kitchen asked, "Do you like to hear that thing beep?"

The tone of his voice indicated that he was getting frustrated.

"What beeping?" I asked innocently.

"Can't you hear that thing beep every time you touch the leads together?" he asked.

After putting the meter within inches of my ear, I could indeed hear it beep. What a surprise!

So began the realization that my hearing was compromised. Years passed, and when I noticed an ad in the newspaper for a free hearing test, I finally decided to get my hearing checked.

I can still remember the young lady who did the test. She printed out the results and took them to her superior. My hearing was good enough to hear her question: "Have you ever seen anyone with hearing like this?" The results looked something like the following:

What this chart means is that at the lower frequencies, I only needed a few decibels to hear the sounds—perhaps a snore in another room or the sound of a spoon dropping on the kitchen floor. But at the higher frequencies, I suddenly needed more than 50 decibels to even perceive the sound. A human talking in normal tones is about 60 decibels. That means that in a normal conversation, I am missing some of the highest pitches. Since most of the human voice is at the lower frequencies, I hear a person's voice and understand it . . . most of the time. But I often find myself saying, "What was that? Can you repeat that?"

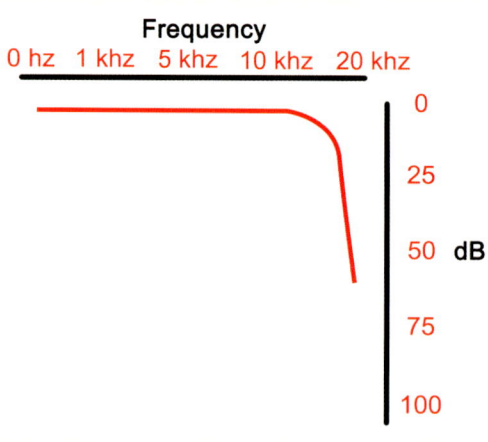

And the birds!

While out in the fields or woods, my son often says, "Did you hear that warbler?" Or, "There's a sparrow in that bush. I can't see it but I hear it."

I have come to realize that I can hear the singing of only about half of the birds. For years and years I had read about warblers but did not know that any were around. Only after I realized that I cannot hear most warblers did I come to understand that, yes, warblers do live in the area. Need I tell you that I am disappointed not to be able to hear them sing?

The culprits

So who or what caused my hearing loss? While it is impossible to know or prove how I came to lose my hearing—perhaps I was born this way—there are some common culprits for hearing loss: headphones or earbuds playing too loudly, table saws and other shop tools, chainsaws, engines without mufflers, guns, and other noise-making machines.

Let's think about the pictures on the next page and the sounds each one produces.

Obviously, you cannot hear anything from a picture in a book, but you may have noticed that the man in the tractor is wearing earmuffs. Very wise! But if we ponder this just a little more, we can conclude that even with the earmuffs, the man in the tractor likely still hears more noise than the man using the horses.

Everything from air conditioners to vacuum sweepers to washing machines bombard our ears with sound. Noise surrounds us. Then, as if that wasn't enough, we turn on some music!

In the workplace, the noise increases even more. Grinders, saws, air compressors, and engines blast our poor ears. It is good to ask ourselves, "Did God intend for people to be exposed to so much noise pollution?"

How sound gets to our brain

A little lesson on the ear can help us understand the science behind noise . . . and what we can do to prevent hearing loss.

Noise is transmitted when it moves like waves through a medium. We are surrounded by air, which is a mixture of gases. Although we cannot see these gases move, they vibrate when sound waves move through them.

As ripples of sound enter our ears, they hit the eardrum, causing it to vibrate. This moves three small bones that tap against the cochlea, which is filled with fluid. The tapping causes the fluid inside the cochlea to move, just like the water in a water balloon will jiggle if you tap on the balloon somewhere.

Tiny hairs line parts of the cochlea. As the fluid in the cochlea vibrates, the hairs bend over. Think of the wind or water moving grass. When the hairs are moved around, they fire off electrical signals to the brain, which then interprets these electrical signals as sounds. Think of the hairs as tiny switches that are turned on when they are moved. Each set of hairs is tuned to a certain frequency and will activate when the fluid in the cochlea is moved at that frequency.

These short paragraphs barely begin to explain the fullness of the wonderful and amazing thing called the ear. Do I need to mention that between the process of hitting the eardrum and getting sent to the brain as an electrical current, the sound can get amplified up to 22 times? Truly our ears are the work of a Master Designer!

How noise damages our ears

What happens when a nice breeze flutters over a hay field? The grasses in the field sway back and forth, but at the end of the day when the breeze has finished, everything stands straight and tall. But what happens if a windstorm hits the field? We may find parts of the hay field lying flat after the storm has passed. The next day we may find that some of the grass in the damaged hay field has sprung back up straight, while other parts of the field are permanently damaged.

This guinea pig cochlea shows damage to some of the cochlear hairs.

So it is with our hearing. Our inner ears were designed to withstand many sounds. But loud and sustained sounds flatten the tiny hairs like a windstorm flattens a hay field. Like grass, these hairs can often straighten themselves up if they are flattened. But when the damage is too much, they—like some of the grass in the hay field—may never straighten up again. In fact, they die.

Between 16,000 and 40,000 of these tiny hairs are in each inner ear. The hairs tuned to the high pitches are positioned within the cochlea to receive the vibrations first, so it is usually those that are the first to be damaged.

The four options

What should we do when we find ourselves in a location where the noise is harmful to our ears? Remember the four Ws:

1. Weaken

The best option is to WEAKEN the noise. This is the best choice because it not only protects your own hearing, but the hearing of anyone else in the same area.

WEAKENING the noise can be as simple as turning down the volume on a headset or speaker. On a tractor or machine with a poor muffler, it may mean replacing the worn-out or cheap muffler with a quality new one. On the construction site, it may mean covering the generator with a wooden box or using longer extension cords to get it away from your work area. When purchasing new tools or machinery, consider the decibel rating and let manufacturers know that this aspect is important to you.

2. Walk

The next option is to walk away from the noise. Obviously, this is not an option in some cases. But if you have the option of moving away, then do so. Are you standing next to the blaring loudspeaker at an auction? Move to another location. Do you have your miter saw set up next to the air compressor at the jobsite? Move the saw.

The arm-length rule is a simple way to determine the acceptable noise level: if you have to raise your voice to be heard when speaking to someone at arm's length, then the noise level is probably above 85 decibels. That is also the level that starts causing ear damage.

3. Wear[1]

If you cannot reduce the noise at the source or move away, then the next option is to wear earmuffs or earplugs. A good set of earmuffs can reduce noise by up to 30 decibels. Check the rating when buying them; some cheaper models reduce noise less than that. However, a good set of earplugs can reduce noise even more than 30 decibels.

When inserting earplugs, it is important to insert them properly. The first step is to roll the earplug tightly, making it as small as possible. When inserting the earplug, use your other hand to pull up on your ear. This straightens out your ear canal, making it easier to insert the plug.

When in extreme noise, use both earplugs and earmuffs. This will give you some added protection, although it will not actually double it as we would think.

4. Wish

I admit that this last warning sign is of my own making. I'm the one, by the way, who often says, "Speak up! I can't hear you!"

Do you know how many times I say that daily? Believe me, it happens more often than I wish it would—probably several times a day. I WISH I could hear my wife when we are riding in a vehicle. I WISH I could clearly hear conversations after church services are over, standing in a crowd. I WISH I could

---

[1]The Weaken, Walk, and Wear signs are part of an instructional program created by dangerousdecibels.org. Used with permission.

hear the warblers sing their praises to God. I WISH I could hear the person on the other end of the telephone conversation. I WISH I could hear a watch beep. I WISH my son would not have to remind me constantly, "Dad, your turn signal is still on; can't you hear it?"

I also WISH I would have had the courage as a teenager to ask my employer to put a better muffler on the Case 2670 tractor that I drove for hours on end. I WISH I would have told him, "I'm sorry, but I can't drive that thing like that, boss. I want to hear the warblers sing when I am 50 years old."

Many things are hard on our hearing—chainsaws with poor mufflers, shotguns blasting clay pigeons, riding for hours in a pickup with the wind whistling past our ears from the open windows, circular saws on construction sites, air compressors . . . the list goes on.

Don't choose to WISH; choose to WEAKEN, WALK, or WEAR!

Did You Know . . .

- 12.5 percent (1 out of 8) of the children in the United States have hearing loss due to noise exposure?[23]

- 22 million workers in the United States are daily exposed to harmful noise levels?[24]

- 80 percent of welders reported a hearing loss in 2007?[25]

- An expert on hearing has estimated that the average 25-year-old carpenter in the United States has the hearing of a 50-year-old?

- Hearing loss has been linked to high blood pressure, faster heart rate, and other heart diseases?

- Hearing loss has also been linked to stress, inefficient work, and emotional instability?

Gun/Hunting Safety

POW!

This story actually happened—to me. It is embarrassing. I am ashamed. Of all the foolish things I have done in my life, this ranks near the top. I share this to aid you in not repeating my folly.

The .22 caliber H & R revolver split the silence of the bedroom. My jaw dropped in disbelief and my hands began to tremble. I had just shot a hole through the window of my brother's house with an "empty" pistol!

My mind whirled in a tumble of thoughts. Hadn't I checked to make sure it was not loaded? Yes, I had opened the loading port and checked. I had then spun the cylinder to see if all six chambers were empty. Seeing nothing, I had cocked the hammer, pointed the gun out the window, and made a practice shot with the empty gun. But now the gun had gone off, leaving a .22-bullet-sized hole in the glass and bearing silent testimony that it had definitely not been empty.

Amid the zigzag of my thoughts, my brother's concerned voice came from the adjoining living room, "What's going on in there?"

Still whirling in disbelief, I went to face my brother. "I—I—just shot a hole through the window. I checked the gun to see if it was empty, but it wasn't."

The embarrassment of the moment was compounded by the fact that my brother and I had grown up around guns and hunting. In fact, shooting was a big part of our life, and our family had been quite involved in hunting and shooting, probably more than any other family in our neighborhood. Our father had taught us gun safety. We had shot thousands of rounds of ammo . . . and now this.

As we discussed the situation, my brother told me he had left the gun loaded in case he needed it quickly for varmint control. But he had kept the one chamber, on which the hammer rested, empty so it would not accidentally go off in case it was dropped. Evidently I had opened the loading port to the only chamber that was empty. I knew enough to spin the cylinder to check to see if the other chambers were loaded, but I had spun it so fast that I had failed to notice that five of the six chambers were loaded. When the cylinder stopped spinning, it defied the 1 in 6 odds and stopped right on the empty spot. Satisfied that the gun was not loaded, I had proceeded to dry fire it . . . and the gun went off.

Thankfully, at the time of my dry-firing test, I had the gun pointed out the window into the open pasture. Previously, I had "tested" the sights by aiming at a horse in the pasture. To this day, thinking of this almost makes me tremble.

But my embarrassment and shame were not over. My brother rented that particular house from a man who was the owner of a big-game hunting guide business. He was also a big-time trophy hunter himself who traveled internationally, filling his place of business with mounted trophies from all over the world. Now I needed to go and confess my deed to such a hunter!

With a bit of trepidation, I drove to the landlord's home to confess what I had done. Finding the man at home, I related my story and then told him I would fix the damaged window. To my great relief, the landlord, the international trophy hunter, laughed it off. "Oh, that's all right. I shot a hole through my house trailer roof one time!"

Although the kindness and understanding of the landlord was a relief, the possibilities of what *could* have happened that day make me nervous to this day, thirty years later.

Discussion

What gun safety violations can you point out in the above story? (Answers on page 186.)

Gun safety rules

- The first thing to do when picking up any gun is to check to see if it is loaded. Every user must do this personally, even if someone else has already checked.

This photo shows the proper method to check if a bolt-action rifle is loaded. Sometimes the shell can stay in the chamber when the bolt is pulled back. This can happen especially if the bolt was never fully locked down. A visual inspection is not enough!

- NEVER, EVER point a gun at anything you do not want to shoot, even if you are 100 percent sure that the gun is unloaded.
- Always unload guns before entering a vehicle or building.
- Never store guns with shells in the chamber or the magazine.
- Use safety locks on triggers if children can access the guns. Ideally, guns should be stored in locked cabinets, although it is understandable that some people may not be able to afford them.
- Never let children play with guns. Children should use BB guns as tools, not toys, and adults should monitor their activity.
- Always store guns and ammunition apart.

- Always be conscious of where you are pointing a gun, especially when walking with other hunters or shooters.
- Never cross a fence with a loaded gun.
- Always bear in mind that the gun may not be functioning properly, especially if it is an older model. I once saw a breech-action shotgun go off just by closing the breech.

Boys and Guns

Larry dreamed of one day shooting his father's Model 60 Marlin. But for now, he would just pretend. Of course, Dad knew nothing of Larry and his older brother John messing with his guns. They were stored in the old pinkish-brown wardrobe in the corner of the utility room. Tucked inside that old piece of furniture were the shotgun and two .22 rifles.

The boys knew Dad didn't want them playing with the guns. When they were little, they had respected that wish. But now, as they approached their teenage years, their boyish curiosity was growing and they were becoming bolder in their liberty. When Dad was away at work the boys would get the guns out of the wardrobe and look through the scopes and try the sights. This progressed into loading the guns and cycling the shells through the gun. They knew better than to actually shoot the guns.

One April day 12-year-old Larry decided to get the guns out while Dad was safely away at work. He dropped the shells into the magazine tube and then proceeded to shuck them out one by one with the bolt. Satisfied that the last shell was out, he placed the end of the barrel on the lower sash of the window and picked out a spot along the creek. Easing the safety off, he prepared to dry fire the rifle.

What happened next could best be described as his heart sinking to his knees as a crashing *Bang!* echoed through the room. Larry suddenly did not feel very well as he realized that he had failed to remove the last shell.

Larry made his way into the main part of the house where his mother was. "Mom, how much does a new window cost?" he asked.

"What? Why?" she asked, wondering about the strange question. As the details emerged, Mom didn't get angry, but she did call Dad at work and let him know what had happened.

When Dad came home, he looked rather grim. Looking at Larry, he handed out the verdict: "You will not touch a gun for six months."

Larry did not have nearly enough money to buy a window.

Twenty years later, Larry has never repeated his mistake. He is thankful that the gun was not pointed at a horse or a neighbor's house—or worse.

The lesson

Both of the above stories about guns discharging through windows happened only about a decade apart. In both situations, the sons were respectful of their fathers and had been given teaching concerning gun safety.

One thing we can learn from these stories is that *boys have a strong fascination with guns.* That fascination can push them to violate the respect they have for their fathers. No, not every boy will succumb to the temptation, but sometimes firearms will tempt boys to the limit.

The solution

The solution is simple: *Lock the guns away, even if you trust your children.* This can be with an expensive gun safe or a simple trigger lock. I used to think of trigger locks  as only a deterrent against theft. But they should also be seen as a safety measure. Someone who should not be messing with the gun will be kept from accidentally pulling the trigger—or purposely pulling it and shooting out a window! In Larry's case, a trigger lock would have prevented an accidental firing.

Don't Fall for Venison!

I know the value of venison. Over the last two years, our freezer has been stocked with a total of around 250 pounds of lean, boned venison. About half of that has come through the use of a tree stand that someone gave us, set up on the back part of the farm. Being a meat hunter, I was happy to fill my tag within one hour on the opening day of gun season, leaving me free to spend the rest of the season doing other work. The tree stand gave me the opportunity to see a nice buck (not the one pictured here, but almost as big) and bag him before he noticed me.

I also know the dangers of hunting from a tree stand. Stories have crept into my life—one here, one there, about so-and-so who fell out of a tree stand. It does not take long to accumulate stories of tree stand falls, with some 3,000 of them occurring in 2018 in the United States, or about eight per day.[26]

But wait! Hunting season is only part of the year. Let's say there are 100 hunting days per year. This means that every day during the hunting season about 30 people fall from a tree stand in the United States—more than one every hour. And those only represent the cases that are reported.

Thankfully, death numbers from tree stand falls are down 50 percent from 2010. As tree stands have become more popular, it seems we are finally realizing that it is very easy to fall out of them. Think of it—thirty per hunting day. That number hits me hard. If I could see videos of just one day's worth of falls, I am sure it would make me respect tree stand safety rules much more consistently.

There is one main tree stand safety rule that stands out above all the rest: *Always use a fall restraint system (FRS),* also known as a full body harness (FBH). When I say *always,* that is exactly what I mean. More explicitly, *do not leave the ground without wearing a restraint system.* About 4 out of 5 tree stand falls occur while the hunter is climbing or lowering himself. Tree stand safety researchers report hearing a common theme from almost all people who have fallen from a tree stand: "I didn't think it would happen to me."

Have you ever said or thought something like that? I have. We say things like, "I've been hunting out of tree stands for years. I haven't fallen once. Never even seriously slipped. Never fallen asleep. I'm careful. It won't happen to me."

If you are thinking those words, be aware that almost everyone who has fallen out of a tree stand thought the exact same thing. And consider the fact that over 80 percent of hunters who fell from a tree stand and were injured or died were *not* wearing a fall restraint system.

First of all, what is a good restraint system? A single safety strap that wraps only around your chest or belly is not adequate, unless you wish to die by hanging. A quality restraint system is designed in such a way that the person who falls can survive for some time without strangling himself. The blood will run to the feet, but by moving the legs, a hunter can keep the blood circulating until help arrives. But with only a single strap wrapped around the chest, the hanging person will be more likely to suffocate.

Once you acquire a restraint system, practice using it. Manufacturers of restraint systems recommend that hunters simulate a hanging position just a few inches off the ground, with help nearby in case something goes wrong. This will give you a feeling of what it is like to hang, and what it would take to get yourself out of the predicament.

If you're using a ladder-type tree stand, use three-point climbing, which means having at least three parts of your body on the ladder at all times: two legs and one arm, or two arms and one leg. Then, when you are safely seated, use a haul line to bring up your gear and supplies. The gun should be unloaded and the broadheads covered. If you use a cell phone, have it on you, as well as a whistle and a flashlight. More than one person has found himself hanging in his safety restraint system, and then found that he could not get out of his predicament.

Check your stand regularly, examining the bolts, straps, and webbing. One tree stand fall that I read about occurred after a hunter checked his tree stand straps, but only by pulling on them with his hand. When he put his full weight on them later, they snapped, and down he went!

Remember, as valuable as venison may be, it is not worth falling for.

How many safety violations can you find in this photo?

Answers: No fall restraint system, not using three-point climbing techniques, and carrying gun instead of pulling it up with rope. Other possible answers include no hunter orange, using non-manufacturer straps, and using a strap to bolster the worn-out original seat.

Sharpen That Knife!

So you have the deer down, or the steer is ready to be butchered. Do any safety issues come to mind?

The first that comes to mind may be the obvious one—don't cut yourself! Can you guess what may be the best safety advice for not cutting yourself while butchering your deer or cow? *Keep the knife sharp!*

While keeping your knife sharp may seem counterintuitive, it is a genuine safety rule. With a dull knife, you have to exert more pressure, and this increases the chances of the knife slipping out of control. A sharp knife should glide almost effortlessly through the meat. If you have to grit your teeth or grunt while cutting, it is past time to sharpen your knife. A dull knife is much more dangerous than a sharp one.

Meat processing safety has more to do with proper care of the meat than it does with cutting yourself while processing it. Again, as in many other safety issues, a little common sense goes a long way. The principles are simple: keep the meat *clean* and *cool*.

While field dressing an animal after a successful hunt, keep the hair, dirt, leaves, intestinal contents, and excess blood off the meat. Do what it takes to keep the meat from getting too warm. This may include moving it into the shade, not transporting it in the trunk of a car on a sunny day, and hanging it up at night so the cool air can move over it. Ideally, the carcass should be kept below 40° F, but sometimes one has to do things that are less than ideal during hunting situations. In general, keep these two words in mind: *clean* and *cool*.

When removing the intestines, keep your eyes open for signs of disease or sickness in the animal. Do the organs look healthy? Do you find pus or swollen areas on the organs? Do you smell any putrid odors? If you find signs of disease or sickness, do not eat the meat.

Wash the carcass if it gets dirty during field dressing or transporting. However, always dry the carcass after washing since bacteria in the water can speed up the spoiling process. Keeping the hide on the carcass during transportation will aid in cleanliness.

Should you age your meat? If you want a variety of opinions, ask a variety of people. Some are convinced that meat must age at least a week, while others are just as sure that it makes absolutely no difference. Whatever your opinion, if you do age your meat, keep it below 40°F.

During the butchering process, cleanliness will cut back on contamination and possible sickness. Proper wrapping and freezing or canning will preserve your meat for the coming months.

Meanwhile, keep that knife sharp while cutting up the meat!

Every butcher has a favorite sharpening system. For stainless steel knives, I have found a Diamond sharpening stone to work best. Whatever method used, remember that a sharp knife is a safer knife.

Road Safety

Three Glasses in a Backpack

Suppose you were hired for a unique job: you would be paid to carry three expensive and fragile glasses all the way around the world—in a backpack. If you made the trip successfully without damaging any of them, you would be paid generously.

How would you prepare for such a task? Would you quickly wrap them in a towel and head out, eager to finish the job and get the paycheck? I doubt it. Most likely you would spend a day or two thinking about how you could pack the fragile items into some kind of hard case and surround them with plenty of soft packing material.

The fact is, you have such a job. Your brain is an easily damaged organ that goes wherever you go. And the average person walks the equivalent of four trips around the earth in his lifetime. Thankfully, God has provided us with an excellent packaging system.

The brain is surrounded by a "packing fluid" called cerebrospinal fluid. This fluid in itself is amazing. It is replaced about four times a day as it flows in and around the brain and the upper part of the spinal column. Imagine placing your fragile glasses in a hard case, then filling the empty areas between the case and the glasses with something like honey or jelly. If the case gets a jolt—such as the backpack slipping off your shoulders and falling to the ground—the glasses can move around within the hard case, but no damage will occur.

However, if you happen to get hit with a car while carrying the glasses, or your backpack falls off your back and goes bouncing down over a steep cliff, you may well lose your job as a glass carrier!

So it is with the brain. There is a limit to what the cerebrospinal fluid can take. A man falling off a ladder and landing headfirst on a concrete floor is very likely to damage his brain.

We do well to recognize the limits of what our brains can take and to avoid unnecessary hits on the head. When the brain gets bounced around too hard within the cerebrospinal fluid, it will make contact with the skull, causing a bruise. This damaged area of the brain must then heal, just like any other bruise on the body. The problem is that we cannot see the damage to the brain without special equipment, so we too often assume all is well.

We know that the brain is the command center for the body. What happens when that command center is damaged? The answer is, "All kinds of things!" When the damage is severe, a person may lose consciousness. But sometimes there is damage even when the recipient of the blow maintains his consciousness. Some damage shows up immediately, while other damage may not show up until several days later. A damaged brain can cause emotional changes in a person. They may not be able to hear right. Their sight may become blurry. They may experience strange tastes in their mouth, and the sense of smell may be disrupted. In short, since the brain is the central command center, the damage can show up in almost any part of the body.

Concussions cannot be put into a neat category, even when the symptoms are the same. A person hit on the left side of the head will probably experience different symptoms than one who is hit on the forehead. A person who is hit hard on the forehead may also experience a bruise on the back of his head, as the brain may move around in the cerebrospinal fluid

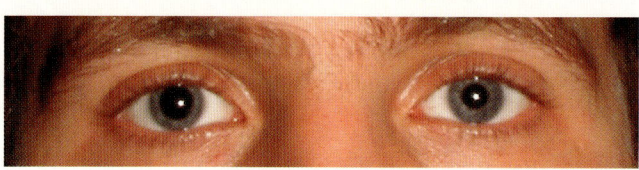

Mismatched pupil size can be an indication of a concussion. This signal is especially useful in small children who cannot tell an adult about a headache or other symptoms of a brain injury.

during the impact, causing more than one bruise. Ultimately, if the impact to the brain is too severe, death will result.

The key to remember is that our brain is an amazing organ, and humans have just barely begun to understand how it works. But it is also very, very fragile. Like the glasses that need to be carried around the world in a backpack, our brain needs careful packaging. And even though our brain has been given to us packaged in cerebrospinal fluid, we need to practice common-sense safety measures to protect it.

Flipped by the Gravel

Fifteen-year-old Emma knew how to handle a bike; she biked everywhere. But as she was returning a neighbor's bike, the gravel on the road did what gravel can do even to good cyclists. As the bike went out from under her, Emma hit the road with her unprotected head.

Waking from the knockout a moment later, she decided to keep going to her destination as no one knew where she was. When she arrived and dropped off the bike, she called her father to come pick her up since she thought she might have a concussion. She was seeing double and her pupils were dilated. Watching his daughter carefully for a while, her father decided she was probably okay and did not need to see a doctor.

Today Emma is a mother. Remembering her scary teenage experience, she teaches her children that wearing a helmet is not a sign of weakness. For her, failing to do so had almost led to a serious head injury. And to make matters worse, no one knew where she had gone. What if it *had* been severe?

TBI facts

Traumatic brain injury (TBI) facts are easier to see than the injury itself. Let's consider a few numbers concerning TBI in the United States:[27]

- Once every 30 seconds someone is treated and released from an emergency room because of a TBI. That's around a million people a year!

- Once every two minutes a person enters an emergency room door and will need to be hospitalized for TBI. Out of these 250,000 people, about 80,000 will have a long-term disability.

- Once every ten minutes, someone in the United States dies from a TBI. That's 50,000 people every year.

When we think of all these sobering numbers, we need to remember that most of these came from accidents of some sort. About half are from motor vehicle crashes, but about 300,000 people a year suffer a TBI from a sports injury. Each year, some 20,000 Americans crack their head too hard while skiing or ice skating. And about 85,000 cyclists will end up in the emergency room because of a TBI. When it comes to powered recreational vehicles (ATVs, go-carts, etc.), around 26,000 people will visit an emergency room each year because of them.

Throwing out numbers like this can numb our minds to the seriousness of the matter. Perhaps the best way to bring the reality home is to count 250 people around you and realize that each year one of these people is likely to suffer a TBI. In ten years, 10 out of the 250 will likely have suffered a TBI.

Yes, it is *that* close to home.

Thinking Deeply and Broadly About Safety

Sometimes practicing safety seems so simple. I mean, if you do not want to experience smashed toes, wear steel-toed boots, right? Simple!

But the issues are not always so simple. In this article, we want to discuss *thinking* about some aspects of safety instead of just absentmindedly obeying a set of safety rules. We will look at one particular safety practice: wearing bicycle helmets. However, we are learning *how to think* about safety more than we are learning about bicycle helmet use.

The question

Let's start with a question. Is using a helmet while cycling a good safety practice?

If you have ever researched the opinions on that question, you already know that opinions range from an emphatic "Yes!" to an equally emphatic "No!" It may surprise you to find out that the ones who are emphatically saying "No!" are not just the teenagers who scoff at wearing a silly helmet while biking. Some reputable bicycling organizations that promote biking safety are also on the "No!" side. At the same time, other reputable safety organizations are on the "Yes!" side.

Why the discrepancy? What does research have to say about the matter? Here is where we need to think broadly about safety issues.

First of all, you will find that it is commonly said—and is indeed proven by studies—that the proper use of a helmet while biking reduces head injuries by 50 percent or more. That could mean that instead of having 100 people per year show up at an emergency room with a head injury from a bicycle accident, only 50 people would show up. This is truly a significant gain and gives solid support to the idea of using a helmet while biking.

Neck injuries

But the matter is broader than a 50 percent drop in the number of head injuries. When it comes to neck injuries, the numbers increase by around 10 percent. So, does that mean we should not wear a helmet since it actually increases the risk of a neck injury? (The reason for this increase is because the helmet makes the size of the head bigger, and if a helmet drags along on the ground during a skid, the helmet is more likely to catch in the dirt and cause the head to twist as the body skids along, injuring the neck.)

Now we have two considerations: a 50 percent decrease in head injuries and a 10 percent increase in neck injuries. But we have to realize that the number of head injuries is significantly greater than the number of neck injuries in bicycle accidents. For example, if there are 100 head injuries a year among cyclists without helmets, there may be only 20 neck injuries. Statistically, if everyone wore helmets the number of neck injuries would rise to 22. However, the number of head injuries would decrease to 50. Therefore, there is an overall advantage of wearing a helmet, even though there would be a slight increase in the number of neck injuries.

Quitters

Did that seem complicated? Wait until you hear this!

When mandatory helmet laws were introduced in Australia in the 1990s, studies found an interesting side effect: the number of bicyclists dropped considerably. Some people do not want to wear a helmet, and they will simply quit biking if they are required to wear a helmet while doing so. The number of bicyclists dropped by up to 30 percent in some areas of Australia after mandatory helmet laws were enacted.

So let's say you have 10,000 bicyclists before a helmet law is enacted. After the law, you now have only 7,000 bicyclists. The number of cracked heads would drop, not only from helmets protecting the heads of the 7,000, but also because you simply have fewer people biking. Sounds like a safer way to go, right?

Not really. What happened to the 3,000 people who quit biking? Well, some of them still needed (or wanted) to go somewhere, but instead of biking, they jumped into a vehicle and drove. Guess what? The chances for getting injured in a car accident are way higher than for getting injured while bicycling. So now many people are actually putting themselves into more danger by getting into a car instead of cycling!

Couch potatoes

But wait, there is yet another aspect to this confusing puzzle. Bicycling is great exercise, and the lack of exercise is a serious health issue in today's modern world. So instead of taking a healthy bike ride, some people will stay at home and sit on the couch eating potato chips and reading a book or watching TV. Some people claim—although it is hard to come up with hard data to prove it—that a person is more likely to have a health issue by sitting on the couch than by riding a bicycle without a helmet!

But hold on a little longer. There is still another aspect. Studies have shown that bikers who wear a helmet are more likely to do dangerous things than those who do not. In practical terms, this means going faster, taking more chances, and doing more stunts. Why? Because they feel safer when they wear a helmet, so they act less safely.

Subconscious thinking

All of these competing aspects may feel a bit crazy, but we still have more to go. A daring researcher in Europe made a study using sophisticated sensors on his bicycle. The sensors could measure precisely how close vehicles were to his bicycle as they passed him. He rode many hours down the road with his bicycle, both with a helmet and without a helmet, to see if the use of a helmet affected how drivers interacted with bicycles. His hunch proved true: vehicles passed on average several inches closer to him when he was wearing

Does the helmet on the biker in the photo subconsciously make him feel more reckless?

a helmet. The assumed reason is that when drivers saw a biker with a helmet, they subconsciously think that the biker is a safer biker than those who do not wear helmets. Therefore, they gave bikers who were not wearing helmets more room as they passed. To be sure, it was only a couple of inches, but the point was clear: drivers give less room to bikers with helmets! (He also put on a wig to see if drivers gave women more room; they did!)[28]

Beware of biking!

Let's look at one final aspect of the matter. When people are constantly told that biking is so dangerous that one needs to wear a helmet while participating, they may discourage children from participating. This effect is similar to those who quit biking because they did not want to bother with a helmet. But the facts are that in the United Kingdom about 10 people per year are killed in bicycle accidents that do not involve a motor vehicle hitting them (which is how most serious bicycle accidents happen). Meanwhile, 350 people under the age of 75 die each year in the UK from falling down a stairs! And about six times as many pedestrians die from getting hit by a vehicle as from getting hit while on a bike.

In other words, bicycling is hardly more dangerous than walking or, for that matter, riding a horse, jogging, or simply living and moving about in a house. However, because of the push to make helmets mandatory, bicycling has gotten the reputation as being dangerous. So dangerous, in fact, that you are sometimes considered crazy if you do not wear a helmet while biking—but you would be considered crazy for wearing a helmet to go up and down a stairway!

Summing it all up

Considering all this, what do we do with the different aspects of bicycle helmet use? Some 20 states in the United States have made it law that minors must wear helmets while riding a bicycle. As mentioned already, everyone—regardless of age—in Australia is required to wear a helmet while bicycling. Meanwhile, many of the reputable bicycling organizations around the world promote the voluntary use of a helmet while biking. But because of the above reasons, many are dead set against the idea of making it mandatory. What is the Christian response to the matter, a response that uses common sense to avoid putting ourselves into unnecessary danger?

I will not tell you what to decide about a bicycle helmet. I want you to think about the matter, consider the various aspects, and make the best decision. One aspect we should not disregard, however, is that if the government does make helmet use mandatory, we should honor that.

But beyond deciding if bicycle helmets are a good thing, I want to encourage us to think about all aspects of safety in a broad way. Think about the long-term aspects. Think about how implementing a safety practice may subconsciously make us take chances we would not normally take, and what we can do to avoid these pitfalls.

Going back to biking helmets, some bicycling organizations say that the most important thing to learn about bicycle safety is *how to avoid getting hit by a vehicle.* After all, if a truck going 55 mph hits you on a bicycle, a helmet is probably not going to make much difference.

To sum up this article—don't just absent-mindedly *follow* safety rules, also *think* about them.

Two-Wheeled Safety

We have delved into some of the competing aspects of bicycle helmet recommendations, but rest assured that safety is not always that complicated. While we want to think deeply about these things, we also want to be able to enjoy a relaxing evening spin on the bike without worrying whether we are doing everything perfectly.

But we do want to be safe! For this reason we will review some safe biking (or scootering) practices that we can carry along with us.

We will start with a few obvious reminders, then progress into more subtle ideas as to how we can arrive home safely from our bike or scooter trip.

- Drive defensively! *Not getting hit* is the most important safety rule. This involves two things: making sure vehicle drivers see you—and that you see them. Always be aware of the traffic. Use a mirror to check up on traffic coming up behind you. *If a vehicle starts passing you in an unsafe situation—when you sense that you are being crowded or you see oncoming traffic—get off the road!*

- Make sure you can be seen. Reflective vests offer great visibility for day or night. Some of these are very lightweight and comfortable, so get into the habit of wearing them anytime you're on the road. Reflectors should also be on the front and rear of the bike and in the spokes for side reflection.

With her brilliant green vest, the bicyclist on the left definitely stands out. Even a slightly distracted driver can hardly miss her! The picture at the right shows the same bicyclist, but the vest, reflector, and white reflective tape have been artificially blackened. Each of these three improves visibility, but the vest is clearly the most effective.

- If you're out at dusk or at night be sure to have adequate lighting, including a bright headlight and a flashing red taillight. Most bicycling accidents occur from 6 to 9 p.m., so be sure to use lights even if it is not quite dark yet. Also be extra careful if you're out later at night, as motorists do not expect to encounter a bike at 1 a.m.

- A mirror is a real safety asset. Use it regularly to check up on traffic approaching from behind. Keep in mind that today's battery-powered vehicles may not make much noise, so use that mirror at all times! Try to stay at the side of the road to give passing vehicles more room. At intersections, however, it is often better to take your place with the traffic, clearly signaling your intentions. Other than at intersections, be slow to demand your right to be on the road. Again, always be aware of traffic behind you, and if necessary, get off the road to allow vehicles to pass. In most cases drivers do not appreciate having to putter along behind a bicycle.

- Always ride with the traffic and in single file. This is opposite from walking, which should be done facing the traffic. Because bikes can go much faster than pedestrians, there are more cases when the bike is going closer to the speed of the traffic. In city traffic, a bicycle can often flow into the traffic.

- Before hitting the road, make sure everything is in working order. Bad brakes or loose handlebars create a hazard, no matter how good the cyclist is. Not only should the equipment be in good working order, everything (seat height and slant, handlebar height, etc.) should be adjusted properly for the rider.

- Avoid the use of a cell phone or a music player while riding or scootering. Our ability to hear important cues, such as an approaching car or dog, may be compromised if we are listening to other sounds. Also, we can easily be distracted by our conversation or audio track.

- Bicyclists are required to obey the same traffic rules as motor vehicles, which means stopping at stop signs, yielding, obeying one-way street restrictions, signaling for turns, etc.

- Avoid riding bikes and scooters on the sidewalks unless the street is simply too dangerous. While riding on the sidewalk is legal in some places, studies show it is twice as dangerous as riding on the roadway.[29] Usually, motorists are not watching the sidewalks as much as they are the roadway, and when a bike or scooter suddenly passes in front of them at a crossing, they are often unprepared. Also, vehicles that are backing out of a driveway do not always check for traffic on the sidewalk.

- No extra riders—period!

- Always carry items in a backpack or strapped on the bike so you can keep both hands on the handlebars.

- Drive a bike or scooter defensively, meaning that you assume that other vehicles do *not* see you, and act accordingly until you are sure that they do.

- When a bicycle or scooter approaches a pedestrian on a sidewalk from behind and wants to pass, you should let the pedestrian know by calling out, "On the left," or, "On the right."

- Watch out for "dooring," which happens when someone in a parked car suddenly flings a door open. In some cities, it is among the most common causes of bicycle accidents, and some people have died from it.

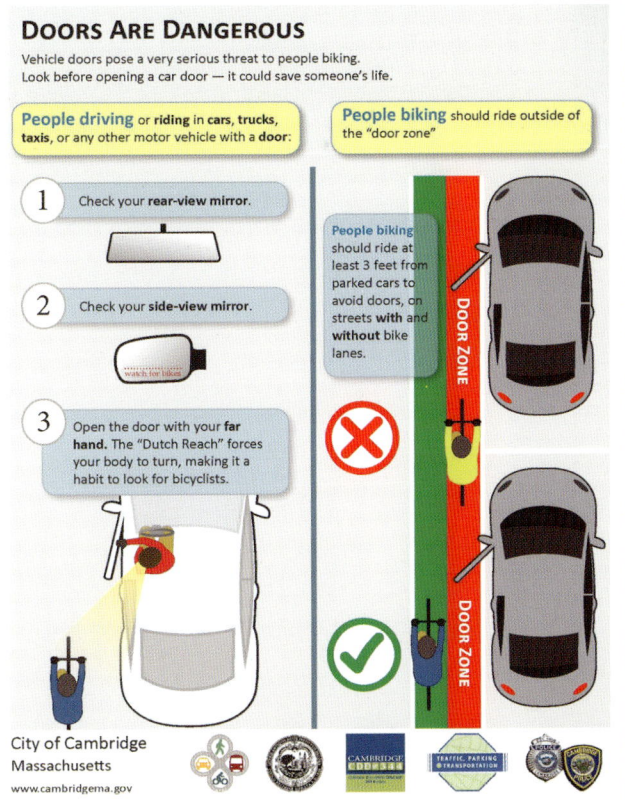

- Motorists should learn and practice what is called the far-hand reach or the Dutch reach. This involves using the hand farthest from the door to open the door. The reasoning for this is that when I am sitting in the driver's seat and use my right hand to open the door, my body has to twist. This twist puts my head into a position that naturally

165

makes me look at the side-view mirror before opening the door and also makes it easier to look over my shoulder to the rear. Try it the next time you are in a vehicle, then practice it from then on! This practice has been used in the Netherlands (hence, Dutch reach) for about 50 years, and several states in the United States have recently added it to their driver education resources.

E-Bikes: More Power = Harder Wrecks

Like it or not, we all have to accept the fact that the faster we are moving when we have an accident, the more likelihood there is of getting hurt. In Holland, where bicycle use is more common among the general public, only 6 percent of bicycle crashes send the rider to the ICU (Intensive Care Unit), while the number jumps to 20 percent for e-bike (electric bike) crashes.[30] Clearly, faster speeds mean greater danger, although other aspects are also at play.

The safety rules for e-bikes begin with the same rules as regular bikes, visibility being one of the most important ones. However, e-bike safety rules do not stop where the regular bike rules do. First of all, an increase in speed means that e-bike users will need to be more alert than ever about approaching danger, as braking times will be longer.

But that's not the only issue. Pedestrians and motorists may not be used to the faster speed of e-bikes, so they may pull in ahead of them or fail to get out of the way. This is especially true on uphill grades, where people are used to thinking of a bicyclist groaning along at just a couple of miles per hour. So imagine their surprise when that "slow" bicycle turns out to be going 25 mph!

The realization of the increase in danger with a faster bike is more important for the biker to learn than for pedestrians and motorists. E-bikers need to remember that most drivers will expect them to be going more slowly, especially when going uphill. It is helpful to think of an e-bike as a mini-vehicle instead of just a powered bike.

If you are using an e-bike, constantly remind yourself, "That motorist probably thinks I am going slower than what I really am." This means the motorist may pass the e-bike, then suddenly make a right turn in front of the bike, not realizing that the bike is right on its tail. Or a motorist or pedestrian may cross the road with the same mindset: "It will take that slow bike 10 seconds to get here; I have plenty of time." But the fact is, the e-bike may arrive in just a few seconds instead of 10.

E-bikes are heavier than a regular bike, which will add even more to the braking time. This extra weight—up to 20 pounds for some models—can also cause mounting and dismounting problems for older people, who latch onto the e-bike idea because of their reduced energy levels. This means that while an e-bike may be helpful to Grandma's mobility, it can also mean a greater chance of a fall while trying to get on the bike. In Canada, a report showed that 70 percent of all e-bike accident victims were men from 65 to 75 years old.

Children should be taught to ride a regular bike well before they are given an e-bike. One person has compared giving an e-bike to an inexperienced bicyclist to giving an inexperienced motorist a sports car with a 700-horsepower engine.

And powered scooters . . .

Every safety principle involving e-bikes equally applies to electric scooters, maybe even more so. Does anyone expect a scooter—the kick-along kind—to scoot along at a blazing 20 mph? But 20 mph kick-along-style e-scooters are the little guys; I read a review about one that can hit 50 mph, with another model claiming a top speed of 56 mph. Does anyone expect a kick-along scooter to go *that* fast? Probably not.

Just as with e-bikes, the unexpected high speed is probably the most important safety concern for electric scooters. It is probably even more important, because if someone sees a person on a scooter out of the corner of his eye, he may not see that the person is riding something—especially something that is moving fast.

When on an electric scooter, think like a driver who assumes a scooter is moving slowly, and then act accordingly.

To motorists

While the operators of e-bikes and electric scooters bear a large responsibility to be extra cautious, all vehicle drivers need to remind themselves that bikes and scooters are no longer just bikes and scooters. They may all look very similar, but some of them are going faster than we might realize. Think twice when passing or making a right turn.
Is this scooter going faster than I think?

Would you expect this scooter to be zipping along at 20 mph or more?

Pedestrian Safety—Mom Was Right!

Pedestrian safety is one of the simpler safety topics. After all, walking down a road is a simple thing to do. So why is it that an average of 17 pedestrians die every day in the United States?

Most pedestrian deaths are the result of being struck by a motor vehicle. As was mentioned in the bicycle safety article, it is far more important to not get hit by a vehicle than it is to pad ourselves in case we do get hit. While the following safety tips may be well known, it is good to review them. We remember things best when we look at them several times.

- Always walk facing traffic if you cannot be on a sidewalk.
- Walk single file and stay close to the edge of the road. Be careful not to go to the extreme of walking on difficult terrain at the edge of the road, which may cause you to lose your balance or trip. A steady step on the roadway may be safer than a tumble at the edge of the road that could send you into the path of a vehicle or send you home with a sprained ankle.
- Avoid using a phone or other electronic device while walking. Some walkers and joggers have the habit of listening to music while exercising. This is a bad habit as it reduces their ability to hear traffic or a snarling dog at their heels.
- Be extra cautious when the sun is low in the morning or evening. At these times, drivers can be blinded by the sun and fail to see pedestrians at the edge of the road.
- In cities, cross the street only at crosswalks. Jaywalking is called jaywalking because in days gone by, *jay* was another word for fool. In other words, a jaywalker is a foolwalker—someone who foolishly crosses the street at places other than crosswalks. Always obey the signals at crossings.

- Be predictable. If everyone practices the same thing, the oddball puts himself into danger by his unique practice. People subconsciously walk on the right side of a sidewalk when there are pedestrians going both directions because we drive on the right side of the road. Be predictable and follow the pattern, even though you have the perfect legal liberty to do otherwise.

- Be seen while walking on the road. This means using light-colored clothing, a reflective vest, and a light at night. Do not wait until the last second to flip on your light at an approaching car. If the driver sees your light a quarter mile up the road, he will have more time to respond properly than if he suddenly realizes that a pedestrian is only a short distance in front of him.

- Mom has told you 50 times already to look both ways before crossing the street, right? Well, just thank her for that good advice and practice it. The number of pedestrians killed in the United States was higher in 2019 than any other year in the last few decades. With faster speed limits and more distracted drivers, Mom's old-fashioned advice is more relevant than ever. Look left-right-left before crossing, and it wouldn't hurt to do it twice on a busy roadway.

- When a car is approaching as you are walking on a road, never assume that the driver has seen you until you make eye contact or see another obvious indication that he has noticed you. Look at the eyes and head of each driver approaching, not just at the vehicle itself.

Avoiding the Grave—Be Seen!

"Everybody wants to go to heaven, but nobody wants to die."[31] Have you ever heard that song?

It is natural to cling to life. Yet sometimes we do things that are foolish and dangerous, making it appear as if we don't care whether we live or die. One example is to risk getting hit by a truck while walking down the road at night. To avoid the grave while walking down a dark road, we need to do our best to let drivers of motor vehicles know that we are there. Consider the following facts about the distance from which a typical driver can spot various items at night:

- Dark clothing: 50 feet
- Medium dark clothing: 80 feet
- Medium light clothing: 120 feet
- White clothing: 180 feet
- Reflective material: 500 feet

In the picture above, the reflective vest shows up clearly even though it is not directly in the headlight beam. And wearing white is definitely better than wearing black.

Carrying a light is even more important than wearing a reflective vest. Even if a car's headlights are not directed at the pedestrian, the light will still be seen.

Pedestrian fatalities are three times higher at night than during the day. I don't think we need an explanation for that. Dusk and dawn are the most dangerous times for pedestrians. In total darkness, drivers are more likely to be on the lookout for something on the road ahead. But with some daylight remaining, they may not be thinking of unseen objects ahead.

Bonus question: Did you notice that the pedestrians are on the wrong side of the road?

No Time to Tie the Horse

"Peter, could you stop and get some milk on your way home from your meeting this evening?"

Of course Peter was willing, so after his meeting he swung his horse and buggy into a neighbor's lane for a quick stop. It was about 9 p.m. A hitching rail was conveniently located right beside the barn door.

Peter usually tied his horse when he got milk, but tonight he was in a hurry. *I really don't need to tie my horse,* he thought. *I'll be right inside the door, and it will take me only about two minutes to grab the milk and come back out.* Besides, the horse was standing in somewhat of a corner between the barn and a playhouse at the end of the barn. If the horse wanted to leave, he would have to make a sharp turn.

So Peter hurried into the milkhouse while the horse was left untied. A couple minutes later, as he turned around to write down how much milk he had gotten, he heard a sound outside. It sounded suspiciously like his horse taking off!

Immediately Peter was out the door. Desperately he reached out to grab the reins. But he was a moment too late, and somehow he missed the reins and the horse took off. Peter has no idea, to this day, what spooked the horse.

The last thing Peter remembers is feeling himself falling and seeing the buggy wheel coming. As he was regaining consciousness, he heard his neighbor talking to him. "Stay down, Peter! Stay down!" But Peter had no idea why he should be lying down, so he sat up. The man was holding a towel against a bleeding wound on Peter's head and had sent his wife into the house for a chair.

Peter was sitting on the chair when he realized that an ambulance was coming. "I'm not hurt that bad; I don't need to go to the hospital," he told them.

But a neighbor girl who had showed up told him, "Peter, for your family's sake you should go to the hospital and get checked out."

Peter finally consented, thinking, "I'll be able to go home in a few hours." Another neighbor who worked for the fire company offered to go tell Peter's wife and take her to the hospital.

When his wife arrived at the emergency room, she told Peter that if they left soon, they would be able to return home with the neighbor who had brought her in. So Peter asked those working in the emergency room, "How long is this going to take?"

No one seemed to know. Meanwhile, they gave Peter a CAT scan. When this was finished, the doctor came in with the report.

"You have a broken vertebra in your neck, your cheekbone is broken in two places, and your jawbone is broken in three places. People like that don't just go home!"

Peter ended up in trauma care for a day and a half and wore a brace for seven weeks. He couldn't eat anything solid for six weeks.

Peter now shakes his head ruefully as he says, "Never, ever leave a horse standing without tying him up—even if you are *sure* he is going to stay!"

SMV—Sign of Multi-Use Versatility?

We all know—or at least *should* know—that an SMV is an emblem (some refer to them as signs or triangles) indicating a slow-moving vehicle. But have you ever seen the same emblem used as a *sign of multi-use versatility?* Driveway markers are one of the popular "versatilities" in which SMV emblems find themselves being employed.

Now is the time to stop using SMV emblems for anything but their real purpose. When SMV emblems are used for other purposes, they begin to lose their original purpose. A person speeding down a rainy road one night may see an SMV emblem at the side of the road ahead. Instead of immediately thinking, "Oh, I had better slow down because a slow-moving vehicle is just ahead," he may think, "There must be a driveway entrance up there."

Placing an SMV sign here slowly erodes the force of its warning for motorists.

Sign of Muted Voice?

We want to avoid using SMV emblems for anything but a warning that a slow-moving vehicle is on the roadway. But have you ever seen them used as a *sign of muted voice?*

This owner of this SMV can only hope that the peeling whiteness in the center will be seen quickly enough to warn that speeding teenager to slow down before he rams his car into the rear of the equipment.

An SMV emblem is supposed to shout out, "Hey, I am going slower than 25 mph, so slow down before you hit me!"

That "shout" of an SMV can be lowered to a "whisper" when we use signs that are peeled, faded, or defaced. An SMV should be bright and reflective enough to "shout" out its warning message.

Sign of Mutilated Visibility

What happens when you trim off part of your SMV emblem so it can fit more neatly onto your machinery? It becomes a *sign of mutilated visibility*. The particular shape and color of an SMV emblem has been standardized for more than 50 years now in the United States. When the color scheme or shape of the emblem is changed, it immediately loses some of its warning power, because consciously and subconsciously that shape and color (and even size) has been engrained into drivers' minds as a warning.

Yes, a full-sized SMV emblem would make life just a bit more unhandy for the owners of this cart when loading and unloading items. But I am sure it would be less unhandy than getting slammed in the rear by a vehicle!

A true SMV

In summary, an SMV sign should only be used to indicate a slow-moving vehicle. Avoid using them for other purposes, and make sure the ones that you do employ are not damaged, trimmed, or faded.

A New Pony Cart

Oh, what joy! Dad had come home with a brand new pony cart. The aluminum bed gleamed in the rays of the late-evening sunshine. The Miller children gathered around, with the younger ones jumping on board immediately while the older ones smiled and called it a goat cart. They had long outgrown a pony cart!

The younger ones begged permission to give it a run, promising to finish their chores first. As Dad headed in to get his supper, he told the children, "No, we don't have an SMV emblem yet."

But the crest-fallen faces worked on his fatherly heart and he relented. A test drive would be fine, he decided, but they needed to stay on the field lanes and off the road. Such cheering!

The busy days on the farm came and went—planting, weeding, and all that comes with spring. The SMV emblem never did get put on, and the children began to do short errands with the new cart. The cart fit Lightning the stallion just perfectly. Lightning was really not a good name for him, because he was not a fast pony.

About a month after the purchase of the new cart, the children wanted to deliver a circle letter to the cousins just down the road. They piled on the pony cart and off they went, with the older sister driving. By this time, no one remembered that it still lacked an SMV emblem.

While the children delivered the circle letter and the baby slept, Mother Martha quickly wrote another letter and took it to the mailbox. On the way back from the box, she stopped to pull some weeds. The sound of sirens filled the air, but as that was not unusual she paid little heed. But more and more sirens sounded, and she could see the lights flashing about half a mile down the road.

Her mind went to her children, but she tried to comfort herself. After all, they had not gone that far down the road. She could see the place where they had gone. So, with a prayer, she returned to her weeding.

A short time later, she heard the *"Beep! Beep! Beep!"* of a horn from a van coming up the road. Recognizing that the driver wanted her attention, she walked to the road. "A pony cart has been hit, and I think it is your children!" the driver informed her.

"Let me get my husband," Martha told the driver. Running to the back of the barn where her husband Paul was running a loader, she told him what had happened, and both of them ran to the waiting van. Although the distance she ran was only 100 yards or so, Martha's heart was beating as if she had run a mile.

Passing the neighbor's place, Martha scanned the driveway for the pony cart but could not see anything. Some of the neighbor children were standing in the yard watching the flashing lights just a bit farther up the road.

Arriving at the scene of the accident, three girls were sitting or lying in the nearby yard, looking dazed but otherwise fine. This included her 8-year-old daughter and two cousins. Martha learned that two of her daughters and two cousins had decided to take the cart farther than originally planned.

The ambulance crew was asking names, ages, birth dates, and other information, so Martha quickly made her way to the ambulance. Inside lay her 2-year-old daughter Emma, not looking well at all. The EMTs later said they were not sure the little girl would make it. But when Martha talked to her, she whimpered and seemed to quiet down some.

Emma was flown by helicopter to a regional hospital, and Martha rode in the ambulance with her 8-year-old to a closer hospital. Other ambulances brought in the cousins. The three were soon released, but Emma spent a few days in intensive care. She had gotten some teeth knocked out and received serious head injuries. The hospital could make no promises on the outcome.

Twelve days later Emma was released from the hospital, but she had to spend another two weeks in rehab. She had to relearn how to swallow, lift her hands, walk, talk, and many other basic functions. She soon healed, except for seizures that started a couple years after the incident. With medicine, the seizures are now under control, and today Emma is a healthy young girl.

The lesson

Don't procrastinate! Put those SMV emblems, flags, and lights on all equipment that will be on the public roadways. The Millers highly recommend putting a flag on a pole on pony carts because the carts sit so low to the ground. They don't know, of course, if an SMV emblem and a flag would have prevented the accident in their particular situation, as the cart was in an open area when an 84-year-old man hit them. But they do know that the civil authorities gave Paul a sentence of community work as a penalty for his negligence in taking proper safety measures.

Others in the community must have taken notice of the accident, because shortly after it happened the local store sold out of pony cart flags!

To Be Seen or Not to Be Seen?

This photograph has a most interesting story behind it. I was on my way to visit the family that provided the previous story about the smashed pony cart. It was a rainy, overcast day, and as I drove along I came upon the wagon in this picture. Since it was heading up a hill, I slowed down, not daring to pass on the hill. Then I noticed that it had one of those cropped-off SMV emblems. "I should take a picture of that for a sample of how not to use SMV emblems," I told myself.

Digging out my camera while I puttered along behind the wagon, I snapped a few

photos. Wouldn't you know? Just as the wagon began to make a left turn across the road into a driveway, a car popped over the hill. You can sense the franticness of the situation in the postures of the boy driving and his adult rider. The pony had already turned his head and likely could not see the car because of the blinder.

Thankfully they were able to get the pony turned back, and the driver of the car saw them in time to slow down. Had the pony continued his turn, things could have gone horribly wrong.

Look at the photo again. See that shiny orange flag? Do you suppose the passengers on the wagon were glad to be seen—to stand out loud and clear? I would guess so.

Humility vs. being noticed

This incident brings to the forefront an important contradiction or tension that we sometimes face. To be safe on the road, it's important to be seen and to stand out in order to avoid accidents. On the other hand, the Bible clearly teaches us to be humble and not to do things to be seen of others.

It is human nature to express pride by drawing attention to ourselves. This can be done by cracking a silly joke, doing a stunt, or by wearing clothes that draw the eyes of others in the wrong way. This can also happen with our vehicles, motorized or non-motorized. This desire to draw the attention of others is why we sometimes see a buggy lit up like a Christmas tree!

So what do we do with this seeming contradiction? How can we emphasize both safety and humility? I think wisdom and common sense will show us the difference between normal safety precautions and decorating our vehicles excessively. That can actually be a safety distraction.

As we work out the tension that can arise between staying humble and practicing safety, we need to consider the aspect of brotherhood. How do others in the church feel? What conclusion can we reach together to be consistent? A brotherhood decision can possibly cut down on people overdoing their lighting in the name of safety.

Then there is the government, which God has ordained to help keep society in order and functioning together. States have valid concerns about safety; killing or crippling someone with a vehicle is emotionally traumatizing, as well as expensive. If I love my neighbor, I will do my part to help him avoid crashing into me. If the civil authorities have concerns about how we are using our equipment and vehicles on the road, we should listen carefully to those concerns and try to find a solution that fits within our desire to walk humbly through this world.

God has called us to love our neighbor and our families. This means we should use prudence and wisdom to protect them. In doing so, safety and humility are not enemies. May we do what we can to live out and promote both of these aspects of the Christian life.

Consistency in Road Safety

The car is full of lively teenagers, laughing and joking. The speakers are thumping along, and the odor of marijuana smoke lingers. As the car rounds a curve, suddenly the following scene presents itself at the outer limits of the headlights.

What is it? Most readers of this book will probably recognize the general outline of a buggy. But what would those who are unfamiliar with horse and buggy transportation think?

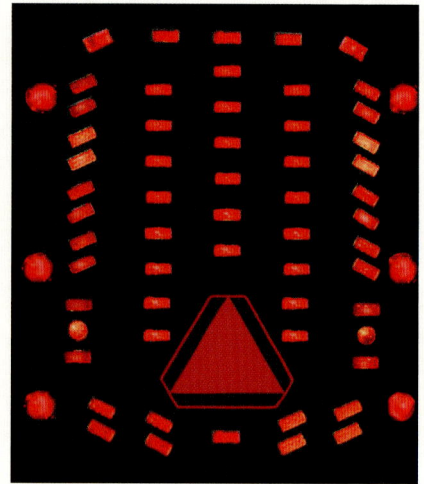

Since the driver of the car has not made a mental connection as to what "it" is, his mind may race through the options as he subconsciously seeks for direction in how to respond. This "it" may be a golf cart, an ATV/UTV, a fast tractor pulling an implement, a horse-drawn vehicle, or just someone who has an odd-shaped load on the back of a pickup truck. The SMV emblem should immediately warn the driver that "it"—whatever it is—travels slower than normal motorized vehicle traffic. But with all the reflectors and lights, the SMV emblem is lost in the tangle and loses at least part of its ability to give a warning.

If the "it" is traveling at 3 mph, then the driver should brake fairly hard. But hitting the brakes hard may cause panic among his lively passengers, or at least cause them to spill their energy drink.

Since the driver is unsure what "it" is, and is also trying to maintain order inside the vehicle, his likely response will be to slow down, but not brake hard, while his mind rushes through the options and seeks for the best response. Part of the problem is that he has never seen anything like this before. "It" is unrecognizable and therefore the driver loses precious response time.

This loss of response time may be compounded by alcohol or drug use, tiredness, sickness, or distraction (talking to someone on a phone or to another person in the vehicle). While these issues are not the fault of the person driving a horse-drawn or other slow-moving vehicle, that fact will not help in preventing a crash. When thinking of doing our part in road safety, we need to think in terms of what *could* happen.

Now let's consider the picture at the top and notice the consistency.

We see some slight differences in the white reflection tape layout and the position of the SMV emblem, but in general, these buggies are consistent enough that if a driver pops over a hill at night and sees one of them, he is likely to immediately think, "Horse-drawn buggy!" This allows him to take *immediate* action for that specific case. He instantly knows what is on the road and can act accordingly.

Across North America, buggy styles and lighting schemes differ. These regional differences are not too big of an issue, though, as most people will become familiar with the regional style near them and subconsciously store that into their brain. The oddball lighting schemes are the confusing ones.

While touching on this topic, let's consider the three items that we see consistently in the above photo.

- **Taillights.** If terrain permits, these lights will be seen before a car's headlights illuminate the SMV emblem and any reflectors, giving an extended warning to approaching drivers that something is on the roadway in front of them.
- **SMV emblem.** These emblems are placed in the same approximate location on the buggies, and they are not surrounded by a myriad of lights. The SMV emblem gives approaching drivers the warning that the buggy is moving slower than normal motorized vehicle traffic.
- **Reflective tape.** This outlines the basic shape of the buggy, giving the motor-vehicle driver an idea of the size and shape of the slow-moving vehicle. Knowing exactly what is in front of him, the driver will feel more secure and in control of the situation.

While consistency will not totally prevent accidents, it can certainly be a big help.

Odd-shaped equipment

What do we do with equipment that is not regularly pulled or driven on the roadways, such as a hay rake, plow, or skid steer? We can still use consistency with the above three-point plan as much as possible. Suppose we are taking a hay rake down the road after dark.

- The rake should have at least one red taillight on it to give drivers as much forewarning as possible that something is on the road ahead.
- A reflective SMV should be on the rear to let drivers know that the equipment is traveling more slowly than normal.
- Either marker lights or reflective tape should indicate the outer perimeter of the equipment. A hay rake deviates in shape from the consistency we see with buggies, but if the two previous points are followed, the driver approaching from the rear only has one-third of the issues to work through.

This last point can be emphasized by the tragic story of a friend of my family who owned a large farm in Indiana. During planting season he was transporting his wide planter (probably a 16- or 24-row) down the highway in the early morning hours. The tractor and planter were both lighted, and an SMV was attached to the rear. There were also marker lights on the planter, but the planter extended several feet beyond the marker lights.

An older gentleman passed the equipment. Not realizing that the equipment was wider than the marker lights, he slammed into it with his vehicle as he passed and was killed. The driver of the tractor also had to suffer: his inaccurately lighted equipment was the cause of another person's death.

Lights vs. reflective material

Thinking of safety, we need to think beyond first impressions sometimes. For example, which would be better to use on a scooter: reflective material or a light? A strip of bright white reflective tape may seem an easy answer. But let's consider the matter a little deeper. As you travel down a road, look at how many items are reflective these days: mailbox numbers, road signs, driveway markers, as well as vehicles and non-motorized transportation. With the high use of reflective material, it can slowly lose its meaning because people become used to seeing it everywhere. There are two lessons in this:

- Do not use reflective material where it is not needed.
- If the option of a light vs. reflective material is available for your scooter, choose the light because fewer people are using lights to mark mailboxes, driveway markers, etc. If a nighttime driver sees reflective material at the side of the road ahead, he may subconsciously ignore it. But he will probably take full notice of a light.

When Being Right Is Dead Right

This tombstone sits somberly in a graveyard near Sandusky, Ohio. The front side gives the name: "Jay C. Smith 1844 – 1929." No details are provided as to exactly how "Little Jay" was right, but the implication is that he was indeed right. Dead right, in fact, and right dead because of it.

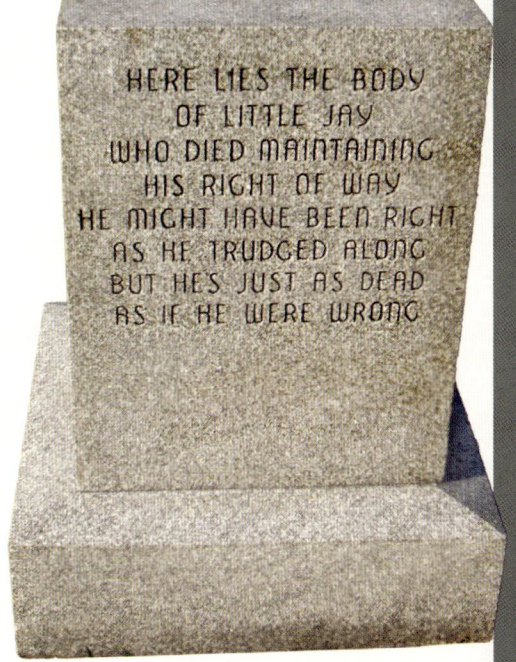

So, when is being right the wrong thing to do? Let's try to imagine Jay trudging down a roadside. One of those new-fangled motorized vehicles—the year is 1929—is careening toward him. "I'm not getting off. I have the right-of-way!" he may have told himself. "Pedestrians have just as much right on the road as anyone else!" And he would have been right. In many law books, pedestrians have the right-of-way. So Jay was right . . . but now he is dead right. It would have been better if Jay had been wrong and assumed that the car had the right-of-way. Remember that we are imagining the story here; we do not know exactly how "Little Jay" died.

When thinking of road safety, it is usually safest to yield even when we think we have the right-of-way. That means stepping off the highway if walking, giving a motorized vehicle more priority than a horse-drawn vehicle or bicycle, and stopping at a crossroad even when there is no yield or stop sign.

It is true—pedestrians do have the right-of-way. Also, unless there is a specific prohibition, horse-drawn vehicles and bicycles have as much right on the road as motorized vehicles. And we all know that roads that do not have stop signs or yield signs have the right-of-way over roads that have stop signs. But don't argue that with a tractor trailer barreling toward you; be wrong for once and give up your right-of-way!

When driving a motorized vehicle, this mindset of giving up one's right is called "defensive driving." This does not mean defending my right; it means defending my life and physical well-being. This same attitude should extend to whatever mode of transportation we are using, be it walking, scootering, biking, horseback, horse-drawn, or motor vehicle.

Do not give someone the opportunity to adorn your tombstone with an epitaph like the one on Little Jay's grave. Go ahead and be wrong; you may just live to tell about it!

Famous last words?
"Don't worry! That speeding log truck is required by state law to give us the right-of-way."

ATV + ROV = 2 Funerals/Day

Have you figured out the equation in the title? It takes just a little math and a little knowledge of off-road vehicles to understand that the funerals from **a**ll-**t**errain **v**ehicles and **r**ecreational **o**ff-highway **v**ehicles number about two every day in the United States. The annual cost for non-fatal injuries from ATVs in the United States totals over $1.4 billion. Yes, *billion!* If you count the fatalities all the way back to 1982 when ATVs started becoming popular, the total deaths accumulate to somewhere around 16,000. Yes, 16,000 funerals and gravestones due to ATVs.

I will not keep you in suspense about how I personally feel about ATVs. (I will include ROVs under ATVs unless indicated.) I would not care one bit—in fact, I would rejoice—if the government banned all of them. On the other hand, I know that some businesses and farms use them responsibly, so I would allow an exception for that. But when I see a trailer loaded with ATVs on a Friday evening headed for some tearing around in the hills, it makes me sad. Are not the woods and streams and fields to be places of quiet contemplation, rather than places for ripping around and roaring like some disgusting behemoth chewing up the trails?

Such fun comes with a price, of course. And sometimes it is the cost of a funeral and gravestone. Yes, websites and promotional materials will tell you repeatedly, "ATVs are not toys." But who listens?

Safety for ATVs starts with, again, common sense. I repeat: ATVs are not toys. If people start ripping and roaring around, expect the funeral rate to rise. Many of the accidents involving ATVs occur on public roadways. In some jurisdictions, ATVs are legal to drive on backroads, but in most cases they are not. Know your local laws. But

What an absolute waste of time, money, energy, and life. Not to mention the common-sense safety rules being broken!

even if they are legal for roadway use, be aware that drivers are not usually expecting to meet one on the road. And if there is a collision with another vehicle, the ATV will usually get the bad end of the deal.

Never haul more people than the vehicle is designed to carry. Be aware that hauling heavy loads can change how the vehicle turns, as well as its balance and stopping distance.

Make sure younger drivers do not try to manage a machine too large for them. While it may be legal for young children to drive an ATV, are they emotionally and mentally mature enough to make decisions at high speeds? One safety organization found that 97 percent of youth under the age of 16 who were injured in an ATV accident were operating a machine that was larger than the manufacturer recommended for their age. Operators under the age of 16 were found to be four times more likely to experience an injury while handling an ATV than those over age 16.

ATV safety organizations recommend wearing a helmet, goggles, gloves, long pants and sleeves, and boots that go over the ankle. This is for sport riding, and business and farm users may find it overbearing for their practical, sensible use.

Like many other young men, I once saw ATVs as exciting. But on one of my first runs, I hit a mailbox. That took some of my excitement—and pride—away, and I am now glad it happened. This was with a three-wheeler, which thankfully manufacturers have stopped making because they are inherently more dangerous than four-wheelers.

But even so, every day two more graves have to be dug, and two more tombstones put in place because of ATVs.

UTV = Upturned Vehicle

Jonas was visiting his neighbors one beautiful spring evening just as the sun was setting. Preparing to head home, Jonas noticed that the neighbor boys had brought out a UTV and a dirt bike to have some fun. As he walked home, the UTV, carrying three boys, and the minibike, carrying one boy, flew past him at full throttle, with the minibike outdoing the UTV. Jonas was concerned about the dirt bike, as it appeared to be going about 40 mph—with no lights. He knew that any little bump or rock could send it rolling. He also knew that the boys had the habit of racing to the end of the field, doing a doughnut turn, and then peeling back to the other end to repeat the process.

As he approached the end of the field, Jonas suddenly heard screams. He could see the lights of the UTV shining upward; somebody was in trouble! Picking up his pace, he arrived at the scene to find an upturned UTV and boys scattered across the ground. One was screaming and holding his arm, while another was groaning and clutching his leg.

The driver of the UTV was fine, and the boy with the injured leg did not appear to be hurt badly. He was limping but was able to walk on the leg. However, the other boy's elbow bones were obviously broken, although the skin was not punctured. At the hospital, they discovered he also had a concussion, which meant a week's stay.

These boys found out too late that in the blink of an eye a UTV can be an **up**t**u**rned **v**ehicle and an ROV can be a **r**olled-**o**ver **v**ehicle. A little speed, a little dirt, a little blast of fun . . . at the cost of a broken arm and a concussion. Thankfully, it did not end as a call for an **u**nder**t**aker **v**isit!

Answers to gun safety violations (pages 145, 146)

- Leaving a gun loaded in the house.

- Pointing the gun at the horse to see how the sights looked, even if the gun was thought to be unloaded.

- Not being thorough enough in checking to see if the gun was loaded.

- Dry firing a gun inside a house, even if it was thought to be unloaded.

Endnotes

[1] https://hcavirginiaphysicians.com/about/newsroom/winter-sports-safety-tips

[2] https://www.cdc.gov/homeandrecreationalsafety/water-safety/waterinjuries-factsheet.html#:~:text=Drowning%20is%20responsible%20for%20more,death%20behind%20motor%20vehicle%20crashes.

[3] https://usatoday.com/story/news/nation/2017/06/26/missing-kids-many-runaways-some-baited-through-technology/103211338/

[4] https://www.nytimes.com/2014/08/16/nyregion/upstate-couple-are-accused-of-kidnapping-amish-sisters.html

[5] https://www.nfpa.org/News-and-Research/Data-research-and-tools/US-Fire-Problem

[6] https://www.usfa.fema.gov/data/statistics/fire_death_rates.html

[7] https://www.cpsc.gov/zhT-CN/node/20425

[8] https://www.nfpa.org/News-and-Research/Data-research-and-tools/US-Fire-Problem/Candle-fires

[9] https://www.grainnet.com/pdf/SummaryofGrainEntrapments2010Steve%20Riedel2.8.11.pdf

[10] https://www.agweb.com/search?fulltext=article+a+steady+march+of+grain+bin+deaths+naa+chris+bennett

[11] https://www.feednavigator.com/Article/2020/03/19/US-Hike-in-grain-entrapment-incidents-last-year

[12] https://www.poison.org/poison-statistics-national

[13] https://www.cdc.gov/niosh/docs/2011-128/pdfs/2011-128.pdf?id=10.26616/NIOSHPUB2011128

[14] https://pubmed.ncbi.nlm.nih.gov/16891944/

[15] https://nasdonline.org/7232/d002442/tractor-overturns.html

[16] https://www.unmc.edu/news.cfm?match=22558

[17] http://counties.agrilife.org/lasalle/files/2011/07/tractor_rollover_4.pdf

[18] https://www.researchgate.net/publication/8672866_Death_by_Chainsaw_Fatal_Kickback_Injuries_to_the_Neck#:~:text=Abstract,28%2C000%20chainsaw%2Drelated%20injures%20annually.

[19] https://incident-prevention.com/ip-articles/the-risks-and-rules-of-chainsaw-operation

[20] https://www.ncbi.nlm.nih.gov/pmc/articles/PMC4154236/

[21] https://www.denenapoints.com/u-s-data-incidence-jack-failure-injury-accidents-nationwide/#:~:text=Our%20Houston%20jack%20failure%20accident%20lawyers%20point%20out%20that%20based,up%20a%20vehicle%20for%20repair.

[22] https://www.hg.org/legal-articles/jack-failures-30320

[23] https://www.hearingloss.org/wp-content/uploads/HLAA_HearingLoss_Facts_Statistics.pdf?pdf=FactStats

[24] https://www.cdc.gov/niosh/topics/noise/default.html#:~:text=Occupational%20hearing%20loss%20is%20one,ototoxic)%20and%20hazardous%20to%20hearing.

[25] https://www.cpwr.com/wp-content/uploads/publications/CB-page-49.pdf

[26] https://www.deerassociation.com/treestand-accidents-can-we-stop-the-insanity/#:~:text=According%20to%20Glen%20Mayhew%2C%20president,2018%20that%20resulted%20in%20injuries.

[27] https://www.cdc.gov/traumaticbraininjury/pubs/tbi_report_to_congress.html#:~:text=Each%20year%20an%20estimated%201.5,50%2C000%20people%20die.

[28] https://helmets.org/walkerstudy.htm

[29] https://www.iihs.org/news/detail/most-e-scooter-rider-injuries-happen-on-sidewalk-study-finds

[30] http://www.copenhagenize.com/2014/02/the-e-bike-sceptic.html

[31] Albert King, "Everybody Wants to Go to Heaven"

Photo Credits

(All photos and graphics not credited are by Mike Atnip.)

Page 7: By Stan Miller at Morguefile image.jpg.

Page 11: By W. R. Grossmith at Wellcome Images, (CC BY 4.0).

Page 15: Wikimedia Commons, public domain.

Page 16: Public domain.

Page 21: Pixabay license, https://pixabay.com/de/photos/koffer-karre-sackkarre-sack-1095854.

Page 22: Peakpx license, free to use.

Page 25: Pxhere.jpg, public domain.

Page 28: Pixabay license, https://pixabay.com/photos/nature-outdoors-fun-bright-summer-3203230/.

Page 31: Flickr photos, https://www.flickr.com/photos/djandywdotcom/30732506203 (CC by 2.0).

Page 33: Adobe Stock, https://stock.adobe.com/images/two-button-disk-cells-batteries/133276055.

Page 35: Adobe Stock, https://stock.adobe.com/images/glass-jars-of-pears-with-a-pressure-cooker/36207707?asset_id=36207707.

Page 38: Adobe Stock, https://stock.adobe.com/images/skaters-on-frozen-lake/136775160.

Page 40: Adobe Stock, https://stock.adobe.com/images/group-of-tourist-vehicle-parking-on-the-frozen-surface-of-lake-baikal-during-sunset-lake-baikal-is-the-largest-freshwater-lake-in-the-world/417749046.

Page 43: Unsplash license, https://unsplash.com/photos/TmA_HPBz6iI.

Page 45: Water-rip-current 1.jpg: CCA-SA by Wikipedia. (Modified by Mike Atnip.)

Page 46: National Weather Service, public information.

Page 48: Photo by Benjamin Beachy.

Page 52: Pixabay license, modified by Mike Atnip, https://pixabay.com/photos/pennsylvania-rural-stand-produce-961488/.

Page 56: Photo by Dmytry Garazha.

Page 59: Public domain, https://commons.wikimedia.org/wiki/File:Harry_Knight_2017-05-28 (Unsplash).jpg.

Page 63: Photos by Veri Ivanova, Unsplash.jpg.

Page 64: FEMA, public domain.

Page 65: Pixabay license, https://pixabay.com/photos/firefighter-emergency-fire-2679283/.

Page 66: U.S. Government, public domain.

Page 67: Official OSHA chart.

Page 70: Pixabay license, https://pixabay.com/images/search/house%20fire/.

Page 74 (bottom): Pixabay license, https://pixabay.com/photos/seven-candles-lit-dark-lighting-1516796/.

Page 76: Pixabay license, https://pixabay.com/photos/room-glass-window-candle-book-2593422/.

Page 77: Photo at Morguefile.com.

Page 83 (top and middle): Public domain.

Page 83 (bottom): Pixabay license, https://pixabay.com/photos/tractor-g%C3%BClle-liquid-manure-spreader-3486266/.

Page 97: Pixabay license, https://pixabay.com/photos/hand-grabbing-taking-orange-child-472244/. (Modified by Mike Atnip.)

Page 99: iStock, https://www.istockphoto.com/vector/customer-service-people-gm588610656-101095217.

Page 100: Pixabay license, https://pixabay.com/vectors/bomb-dynamite-explosives-explosion-157150/.

Page 103: Photo courtesy of Berry Machinery. Used by permission.

Page 104: Pixabay license, https://pixabay.com/photos/machine-soil-tractor-industry-3211667/.

Page 106: Adobe Stock, https://stock.adobe.com/images/small-scale-farming-with-tractor-and-plow-in-field/40615281.

Page 107: Photo by Bobby Miller.

Page 111: CC-by-SA by Wikipedia user Михаило Јовановић. (Modified by Mike Atnip and released under the same license.)

Page 113: Public domain.

Page 116: Public domain.

Page 121: Pixabay license, https://pixabay.com/photos/wheelchair-disability-paraplegic-1595794/.

Page 133: Unsplash license, https://unsplash.com/photos/IZ25OGCuBFU.

Page 141 (top): Pixabay license, https://pixabay.com/photos/vine-tractor-agricultural-machinery-1367155/.

Page 142: From dangerousdecibels.org. Used by permission.

Page 143 (top two): From dangerousdecibels.org. Used by permission.

Page 145: Pixabay license, https://pixabay.com/en/glass-shot-bullet-hole-torn-3249420/.

Page 149: iStock, https://www.istockphoto.com/photo/shotgun-locked-gm116275043-4983604.

Page 155: Public domain.

Page 156: CC-by-SA, Wikipedia, https://en.wikipedia.org/wiki/File:Anizokoria.

Page 157: Pixabay license, https://pixabay.com/photos/bicycle-tires-profile-mature-bike-4159456/.

Page 160: Unsplash license, Thinking-marc-sendra-martorell-unsplash.jpg.

Page 162: Public domain.

Page 165 (bottom): City of Cambridge, MA. Used by permission.

Page 167: Unsplash license, https://unsplash.com/photos/wt2Wsq0Cox8.

Page 168: Public domain.

Page 171: Adobe Stock, https://stock.adobe.com/images/amish-buggy-with-wagon-hitched-to-rail/269051461?asset_id=269051461.

Page 172 (top): Public domain.

Page 174: Adobe Stock, https://stock.adobe.com/images/amish-horse-buggy-107/279523346.

Page 181: Public domain.

Page 182: CC-by-A, Oregon Department of Transportation, https://commons.wikimedia.org/wiki/File:Log_truck_(5494951495).jpg.

Page 183: Pixabay license, https://pixabay.com/photos/atv-quad-drive-dust-gravel-tire-3604068/.

About the Author

Mike Atnip grew up among the cornfields of east-central Indiana, tromping through the fields and woods on a regular basis. His wife Ellen grew up in southeastern Pennsylvania, at the foot of Blue Mountain, but later lived in northern New York where the snow blows deep. Mike and Ellen have one son, Daniel, who was adopted from the tall Andes Mountains in Bolivia, South America, but has lived most of his life in the United States.

Over the years, Mike has been involved in a variety of occupations, which helped him as he gathered material for this book.

Mike welcomes reader response and can be contacted at atnips@gmail.com. You may also write to him in care of Christian Aid Ministries, P.O. Box 360, Berlin, Ohio 44610.

About Christian Aid Ministries

Christian Aid Ministries was founded in 1981 as a nonprofit, tax-exempt 501(c)(3) organization. Its primary purpose is to provide a trustworthy and efficient channel for Amish, Mennonite, and other conservative Anabaptist groups and individuals to minister to physical and spiritual needs around the world. This is in response to the command to ". . . do good unto all men, especially unto them who are of the household of faith" (Galatians 6:10).

CAM supporters provide millions of pounds of food, clothing, Bibles, medicines, and other aid each year. Supporters' funds also help victims of disasters in the U.S. and abroad, put up Gospel billboards in the U.S., and provide Biblical teaching and self-help resources. CAM's main purposes for providing aid are to help and encourage God's people and bring the Gospel to a lost and dying world.